To
Professor Lin Tongji

獻給林同濟教授

Translated by
Wu Juntao 吳鈞陶譯

杜甫詩新譯 *Tu Fu-A New Translation*

The Commercial Press, Ltd.

杜甫詩新譯
TU FU-A NEW TRANSLATION
Translated by WU JUNTAO
Published by
THE COMMERCIAL PRESS, LTD.
35 Queen's Road, C. Hong Kong
Printed by
C & C JOINT PRINTING CO., (H.K.) LTD.
75, Pau Chung Street, Kowloon, Hong Kong.
First Edition July 1981

ISBN 962 07 1012 6

杜甫像

CONTENTS

目 錄

Front-piece: Tu Fu *by Zhang Renci*
10 Illustrations *by Tao Xuehua and Yang Lilu*

卷首杜甫肖像（作者張紉慈）
插圖十幅（作者陶雪華，楊利祿）

Tu Fu - A New Translation

From the Translator

I began the translation in 1974, when China was still under the misrule of "the gang of four". It was a time of disaster, and like most intellectuals, I lived without hope, without future. Books, and the permitted ones at that, were the only friends one could safely communicate with. Fortunately, some of my books had been returned to me after the so called domiciliary visit at the beginning (1966) of the Cultural Revolution, which was indeed an event "without parallel in history".

Tu Fu, the great poet of ancient China, was then absurdly considered as a reactionary Confucianist; nevertheless, I made friends with his poetry for many a bleak, lonely and tedious night. I read and re-read, and tried to translate some of his poems, partly for the practice of my English and partly for finding myself a refuge from my pangs. I even occasionally dreamed dimly that the lucubrations might some day bring me better circumstances, if ever the day should come and the dark clouds roll by.

In a fancy world, I rambled like a pilgrim in the fane of Tu Fu, prayed before his shrine for revelation, conjured the inspirations to shower on me and enable me to creditably

譯者的話

我於一九七四年開始翻譯這本書，那時還是稱做“四人幫”統治時期。那是一場浩劫，而我像大多數知識分子一樣，在沒有希望和前途的境地中生活。書籍，而且是只有被允許閱讀的書籍，才是可以與之安全地交往的唯一的朋友。幸運的是，我的一部份書籍已經還給了我。這些書籍是在一九六六年文化大革命開始後所謂抄家的時候抄去的。這場浩劫眞是“史無前例”的事。

杜甫，這位中國古代的大詩人，當時被荒謬地看做反動的儒家。雖然如此，在許多許多個黑暗、孤獨和睏倦的夜裏，我還是和他交朋友。我反覆閱讀，試着翻譯他的一些詩篇，一則爲了鍛煉自己的英語；一則爲了在苦難的現實中替自己尋找一個隱避所在。我有時甚至模糊地夢想這種焚膏兀兀的勞作，有一天能帶給我較好的處境，如果這一天在烏雲散去以後，竟然到來。

於是，在一個幻想的世界裏，我像是一個虔敬的香客，躑躅在杜甫的廟堂裏，在他的神龕前祈求他的啟示，祝禱靈感能像醍醐灌頂，使我能夠恰當地把他的思想、

put his thoughts, feelings and art, so brilliantly embedded in his verses into some sort of readable English.

Art is a balm to one's soul —— I am positively convinced of that, especially when it is the art of Tu Fu, a kind, humane, amiable, but suffering genius. He gave me peace and ease. He offered me companionship. Again and again I was charmed and taken by surprise by the magic of his pen. But it was not an easy task to convey what I felt to others with my pen in another tongue. I scrutinized every line and every letter with their multiple meanings and nuances, and fumbled in the maze of English words and sentences to find what I thought suitable. Years passed. More and more of my hair turned grey as the manuscripts piled higher and higher. I could not refrain from heaving a sigh of relief when I came to the end of the stack at last, yet I am eager to know from my readers if I have done something worthy in some way or other.

It is said that poetry can never be adequately rendered in another language. Be that as it may, various versions are allowable, and even necessary. The poetry of a great poet invites different translators just as a beautiful scenery invites different painters to paint. I knew little about the various translations of Tu Fu when I started mine. It was then difficult to obtain any. I got some of them afterwards. I pay my regards to foreign sinologists and Chinese scholars for their merits, and pray, as a new-comer, I might join the line.

感情和藝術移植到可以一讀的英語中去。他的這一切是精彩絕倫地表現在古漢語的詩句之中。

藝術是心靈的香膏——我確實相信這一點，特別是杜甫這位忠厚善良、却又顚連不幸的天才的藝術。他給了我心靈上的和平與安甯。他給了我友誼的溫暖。我一再因他神奇的妙筆而沉醉，而驚嘆。可是，把我的感受用我的筆以另一種文字傳達給別人，却非易事。我研讀着每一行，每一個字，辨別其多種多樣的含義和細微之處;然後在英語的詞句的迷宮中尋找我覺得合適的材料。年復一年地過去，隨着白髮漸增，我的稿紙也越積越多了。到現在終於搬掉了一座大山，我不禁如釋重負，長吁一聲。可是我仍然急於從讀者們那兒知道，我是否做了一件在某些方面還有點價值的工作。

據說詩歌决不能妥貼地譯成另一種文字。正因如此，各種譯本應是允許的，甚至必需的。一位大詩人的作品可以讓不同的譯者翻譯，正像美景可以讓不同的畫家臨摹一樣。我着手翻譯杜詩的時候,各種翻譯看到的很少,因爲當時很難得到一本。後來設法看到一些。我向外國的漢學家們和我國的學者們的功績致敬，同時希望自己作爲一個新手，能夠忝附驥尾。文化遺產屬於所有的民族和所有的時代。在這個紛紛擾擾的世界上，在人類的大家庭裏，讓這種共有的遺產的分享使我們明瞭“四海

Cultural heritage belongs to all nations and all eras. In this troublous world, let the sharing of our mutual heritage make us aware that in the human family "all men are brothers".

As to the prosody, I have tried my best in keeping to the rules of metre, rhyme, rhythm etc. at those places I found possible. I have no compunctions in letting them go whenever I come to my tether's end. I was advised once and again that I had better abandon the rules since it was a thankless job. But I am a lover of music and melody in my own way and it was hard for me to part with them. I believe it is the privilege of poetry to have rhyme and rhythm (I think metre too) as much as it is the privilege of a girl to fondle flowers and of flowers to have colours and fragrance. It was a great finding when man first used rhyme and rhythm, and what is the use of them if even poetry would leave them alone? And my lack of skill has not dissuaded me from my attempts.

Tu Fu has left to the world more than one thousand and four hundred poems. In the present collection one finds less than one tenth, and not including all of his famous ones. I only regret that the perpetual wheel of work and routine has prevented me from translating all I want to translate. There must be a stop to everything, and I have to suspend my pen for the moment.

It is a miracle that the book is actually published. If the reign of "the gang of four" should still be with us my manu-

之內皆兄弟”的事實吧。

至於格律方面，我在自己認爲可能的地方，都盡力使用了音步、押韻和節奏等的規則；又不惜在無法可想地方聽其自然。别人一再勸告我最好放棄這些規則，因爲這是勞而無功的事。可是我愛好音樂和旋律，要教我抛開這些東西，眞有些爲難。我覺得押韻和節奏（音步亦然）是詩歌的特權，正像鮮花是女孩子的特權，芬芳是鮮花的特權一樣。人開始使用押韻和節奏的時候是一種偉大的發現；要是連詩歌也抛棄這些東西，它們還有甚麼用處呢？儘管我自己欠缺這方面的技藝，也沒有放棄這一嘗試。

杜甫留給後世一千四百多首詩歌。在這本集子裏收了不到十分之一，還不包括他所有的名篇。遺憾的是工作和日常瑣事的永動輪不允許我翻譯出我想翻譯的那許多。任何事情都得有個結束，我不得不在此刻擱起筆來。

這本書竟然得到出版機會實在是一個奇迹。如果還是“四人幫”統治我們，我的稿件必然是一堆廢紙。的

scripts would surely be wastepapers. It is a fortune indeed that I should have been introduced by Comrade Chen Bochui, a venerable writer of juvenile literature, to Comrade Yeh Junjian, a well-known writer of many Chinese and English books.

I take this opportunity to express my gratitude to Mr. Lee Cho Jat, the chief of The Commercial Press, Hong Kong Office, and the editor Mr. Lo Chi Hong, who accepted my work immediately upon Comrade Yeh Junjian's recommendation.

Acknowledgements are owing to many others who have read my manuscripts, corrected my errors, or given me good counsels. Among them are Professor Lin Tongji, and Comrade Yang Zhihong. If mistakes still remain, it is only because I was often too dogged to accept their advice. Be it as it may, I beg for comments from readers and shall be so much the wiser in the revised edition.

I cannot finish without mentioning the firm support from my wife who, for many years, suffered what I suffered and hoped what I hoped.

Wu Juntao

April, 1980, Shanghai.

確幸運，我終於由那位年高德劭的兒童文學作家陳伯吹同志介紹給葉君健同志，他是名作家，寫過好多本中、英文小說。

我要借此機會表示感謝商務印書館香港辦事處主任李祖澤先生和編輯羅志雄先生;經過葉君健同志的推薦，他們立即接受了我的稿件。

還要感謝其他許多同志，他們審閱原稿,指正錯誤，或者賜與很好的意見。主要有林同濟教授和楊之宏同志。如果仍然遺留了錯誤，那僅僅是因爲我固執己見，不聽勸告所致。因此之故，我請求讀者們賜教，以便再版時有所提高。

我必須在結束的時候提一提我妻子給我的一貫的支持。許多年來，她遭受着我所遭受的事，希望着我所希望的事。

吳鈞陶

1980年 4 月，上海

Tu Fu, A Short Biography

Tu Fu (712 – 770), alias Zimei, sometimes called himself "An Oldster of Shaoling" or "A Commoner of Tuling" according to the place on the outskirt of Chang-an where he had once lived, has also been called by later generations as Tu, the Left-Hand Censor or Tu, The Councillor of the Ministry of Works which was his official title.

Coming of good descent, he was proud of his remote ancestors Tu Yu, a famous general and historian; his great-grandfather Tu Yiyi, a magistrate of Gong County in Henan Province (the birth-place of Tu Fu); his grandfather Tu Shenyan, a well-known poet of the early Tang Dynasty as well as scholar and high official; and his father Tu Xian, Vice-Magistrate of Yanzhou and Magistrate of Fengtian County.

Death bereaved him of his mother early in his childhood, Tu Fu became an orphan, and his father sent him to Luoyang (the East Capital) to be in ward to his second aunt. His stepmother gave birth to several children afterwards. He was weak but talented and he wrote poetry and was skilled in calligraphy when he was not yet ten years old.

In 731 – 740, the young man twice made the long journey

杜甫小傳

杜甫（公元712年——770年），字子美；由於曾居住在長安城南少陵和杜陵一帶，有時自稱"少陵野老"或"杜陵布衣"。後人按照他的官銜也稱他杜左拾遺或杜（檢校）工部（員外郎）。

他對於自己出身名門，引以爲榮。他的遠祖杜預是西晋時有名的大將和歷史學者，注解過《左傳》。曾祖父杜依藝是鞏縣（在今河南省）縣令。（杜甫的誕生地便是鞏縣。）祖父杜審言是唐朝初期的著名詩人，武則天時做過膳部員外郎，又曾任修文館直學士。父親杜閑曾任兖州（在今山東省）司馬及奉天縣(今陝西省乾縣)縣令。

杜甫的母親在杜甫年幼時便已亡故，父親把他送到東都洛陽他的第二個姑母家寄養。父親續弦以後，後母生了幾個孩子。杜甫幼年時身體虛弱，但很聰明，還不到十歲便學寫詩歌，嫻於書法。

公元七三一年至七四〇年之間，杜甫作了二次長途

through the east and north of China; he traveled in Jiangsu, Zhejiang, Henan, Hebei and Shandong provinces. The poems "Looking at the Mountain Tai" etc. were the records of that period.

About in 741, when Tu Fu was thirty years old (according to Chinese way of counting the age), he married Miss Yang, a daughter of the Vice-Minister of Agriculture Yang Yi. We know only the surname of Tu Fu's wife, because in feudal China there was no place for woman either in society, or in books. They got on well with each other during their lifetime, but in Tu Fu's collections we can find only a few poems written specially for his wife.

In 744, in Luoyang, Tu Fu met Li Po (701 – 762), another great poet that China has ever had. Genius is rare in any age; it is even a golden chance that the two geniuses should come together. They became fast friends at the first meeting, as though they were conscious that in the future they would shine forever like Gemini in the sphere of literature. They travelled, drank and hunted with Gao Shi (702 – 765), also a poet. They sent poems to each other afterwards, among those of Tu Fu to Li Po, there are "Dreaming of Li Po, Two Stanzas" and "At the End of the World I think of Li Po".

In 746, when Tu Fu was thirty five, he came to Chang-an, the Capital (or West Capital) and the largest city at that day. In ancient China, no profession was honourable for the in-

旅行，漫遊中國東部和北部地區，到過現在的江蘇、浙江、河南、河北和山東各省。《望嶽》等詩篇便是他那一時期的記錄。

大約七四一年，杜甫三十歲的時候，和司農少卿楊怡的女兒結婚。我們只知道杜甫的妻子姓楊，不知道她的名字，因爲在中國封建社會裏，一般婦女在社會上和書本上都沒有地位。他們一生相處很好，可是在杜甫的詩集裏寫給他的妻子的作品不多。

七四四年，杜甫和李白在洛陽相見。李白（公元七〇一年——七六二年）是中國文學史上另一位大詩人。天才在任何時代都是稀有的；兩位天才的相遇眞是千載難逢的幸會。他們一見如故，彷佛知道他們將來會在文學的星空像雙子星座那樣永放光芒。他們和另一位詩人高適（公元七〇二年——七六五年）一起漫遊、飲酒和打獵。他們後來互贈詩歌。在杜甫給李白的一些作品中，有《夢李白二首》和《天末懷李白》。

七四六年，杜甫三十五歲時，來到首都長安（或稱西都），那是當時最大的城市。在古代中國，對於知識分子來說，沒有什麼職業比做官更爲尊貴的了。“學而

tellectual other than being an official. "He will make an official who learns well" was the traditional creed, and also an unquenchable desire of Tu Fu. He wrote letters and poems to influential officials, asking them to elevate him from humbleness. He even presented directly to Emperor Xuanzong the poetical proses on the *Three Rites*, the *Worship of Heaven on the Summit of West Mountain* and on the *Vulture.* He attended the imperial examination, which was a system of selecting officials. His efforts over some ten years proved in vain, and was stricken with illness and poverty. Tu Fu had to be "a vender of herbs in the streets and eat salt with my friends", and bought rice at reduced price from the Emperor's warehouse for a certain time. His elder son Tu Zongwen was born in 750, and the younger Tu Zongwu in 753. Unable to afford his family to live in the Capital, Tu Fu sent his wife and children to Fengxian County, where his third infant child was even starved to death afterwards.

It was not till 755, when forty four years old, that Tu Fu gained a low position as Commissary Recorder in charge of the weapons and keys in a yamen.

Before his fortieth year, Tu Fu left but some fifty poems; "A Painting of an Eagle" and "The Chariots Rattle On" are among the best.

The vortex of a historical event created a turmoil. Two Tartar generals An Lushan and Shi Siming rebelled against

優則仕”是傳統的信條，也是杜甫始終熱烈懷有的願望。他寫了一封封信、一首首詩給權貴們，希求他們把他從貧寒中提拔上來。他甚至於直接向玄宗皇帝獻上了《三大禮賦》、《封西岳賦》和《鵰賦》。他還參加了殿試，這是選拔官吏的一種制度。他的十來年的努力結果是一事無成，却貧病交加。有一個時期他不得不“賣藥都市，寄食友朋”，天天從皇帝的太倉裏買平價米。他的長子宗文生於七五〇年，次子宗武生於七五三年。杜甫無力負擔全家在長安的生活費用，只得把妻子和兒子送到奉先縣（今陝西蒲城）寄居。後來他的第三個兒子在未滿周歲的時候在那兒餓死。

直到七五五年杜甫四十四歲時才得到一個正八品下的小官，那是“右衞率府胄曹參軍”，任務是看守兵甲器器仗，掌管門禁鎖鑰。

杜甫四十歲以前的詩作只留下五十來首。《畫鷹》及《兵車行》都是他的佳作。

一件歷史性事件的漩渦引起了一場騷亂。蕃將安祿山和史思明反叛唐朝統治，於七五五年年底發動戰爭，

the reign of the Tang Dynasty; they started a war at the end of 755 which lasted for seven years before it was crushed down. It was a turning point marking the Tang Dynasty's decline from its summit, and it brought Tu Fu a new chapter of his life too.

As the rebels pressed on towards the Capital, Emperor Xuanzong fled far away into Sichuan Province. So the tragedy happened on the way when he killed his favourite concubine Yang Yuhuan. The Heir Apparent took accession to the throne, entitled himself Suzong in Lingwu County, and moved to Fengxiang County later on.

In 756, Tu Fu ran away with his family to Fuzhou. Settling down in a temporary dwelling at the suburban Qiang Village, he, cherishing with heroic loyalty his devotion to the emperor and country, went alone in the chaotic situation to Lingwu County. Unfortunately he was captured half-way by An Lushan's soldiers, and escorted to Chang-an. For eight months he lived with anxieties in the enemy-occupied Capital, he wrote "The Moonlit Night", "A Spring View" etc.

He escaped at last and ran all the way to Fengxiang. He prostrated himself in his shabby clothes with elbows sticking out and a pair of gunny shoes before Emperor Suzong. He was appointed at once the Left-Hand Censor, and advisory official of the emperor. It was not an unimportant post although still low in official rank. But before long he was

延續七年多才平定下來。這一事件是唐朝由盛到衰的轉折點，也給杜甫的生活帶來了新的一章。

叛亂逼進首都的時候，玄宗遠避入蜀。半路上發生了處死貴妃楊玉環的慘劇。太子李亨，號肅宗，於七五六年在靈武縣即位。後來遷往鳳翔縣。

七五六年，杜甫一家逃到鄜州。他把家暫時安置在城北的羌村，自己懷着忠君報國的英雄氣概，在混亂的局勢中，隻身冒險奔往靈武縣。不幸的是半路上被安祿山的部下逮捕了，押送到長安。他帶着不勝焦急的心情在這敵人佔領的首都躭了八個月，寫了《月夜》及《春望》等詩篇。

他終於逃出來，一路奔到鳳翔縣。他穿着袖露兩肘的破衣衫，脚穿麻鞋，匍匐在"天子"肅宗的面前。肅宗立即任命他爲左拾遺。這是"從八品上"的官職，職務是供奉皇帝，向皇帝提供意見。這不是一個不重要的職位，雖然官階仍然是低的。可是不久他便得不到肅宗的器重，因爲他誠懇坦率，忠於職守，爲被貶謫的宰相

detested by the emperor because he was honest, frank and faithful in discharging his duties and he spoke well of Prime Minister Fang Guan who was then demoted. The intense words he used in the memorandum enraged the emperor so much that Tu Fu was handed over for interrogation. He proved to be innocent at the end of it, but he was henceforth disappointed in politics.

In the autumn of 757 when the capital was recaptured, Tu Fu went back there with his family. He had a comparatively peaceful and leisurely time for less than a year. He wrote "The Winding River, Two Stanzas" etc.

In the Sixth Moon of 758, Fang Guan was demoted once again, and Tu Fu, being considered as one of his party, was also demoted to Huazhou County to be a Minister of Education there.

He came to Huazhou in the hot summer, worked hard, burying himself among the official documents, and then resigned one year later.

During this period, he went to Luoyang to have a look at the place where he had lived in his childhood. The place was ravaged both by the rebellious army and Huihe (Ouigour), the tribes whom Emperor Suzong allowed to loot, on the condition of helping him to recapture the two capital . The desolate and dilapidated view met Tu Fu's eyes; the disasters

房琯辯護。他上疏皇上，言詞激烈，甚至於使肅宗下令審訊。審訊結果，證明無罪。雖然如此，他却從此以後失意於仕途。

七五七年的秋天，首都光復，杜甫帶着家人回到這裏。在不到一年的時間裏，他有着比較安靜和悠閑的日子。他寫了《曲江二首》等詩。

七五八年六月，房琯再次貶官。杜甫被認爲屬於房琯一伙，也外貶爲華州司功參軍，管理文化教育工作。

他在炎熱的夏季來到華州，辛勤工作，埋頭在成堆的文牘之中，做了一年便毅然棄官。

這一時期，他回到過他童年時代居住過的洛陽。這地方遭到叛軍和回紇軍兩方面的蹂躪。肅宗曾經應允回紇人，如果協助收復兩京，可以任憑他們在當地劫掠。杜甫極目所見是荒蕪倒敗的慘狀。倖存者遭受的災難和困苦深深打動着他的心。在此亂世中他不期在洛陽遇見了他年輕時的故交衞八處士。他帶着驚喜交集的心情爲

and sufferings of the survivors struck Tu Fu's heart; so he wrote a poem to Hermit Wei, expressing his feelings of hilarity mixed with surprise when he found out his old friend in Luoyang amidst the turbulent times, and wrote the brilliant set of poems — "The Three Officials" and "The Three Partings", showing his deep sympathy with the people.

It is said in the ancient history book "A New History of the Tang Dynasty" that local famine made Tu Fu decide to leave Huazhou; but it is thought that the dim prospect of his political career confirmed his resolution too.

In the Seventh Moon, 759, Tu Fu took a long journey with his family, climed over a two-thousand-metre high mountain Long, came to Qinzhou (now in Gansu Province) where his nephew Tu Zuo lived. Tu Fu stayed there for about four months only, because the financial help from his relatives and friends, and the sale of herbs could hardly support him that he had only one copper left in his pocket. On top of it, a fit of malaria took hold of him at the same time.

A letter from the magistrate of Tonggu County came in time, inviting him to live there. He heard from others that it was a blessed spot and was full of yams, bamboo shoots and honey. But as the incident revealed itself, Tu Fu had gone farther and fared worse. After overcoming the dangers and struggling along precarious mountainous paths through the crags and braving the roars of beasts, the family arrived at

他寫了一首詩《贈衞八處士》。他又寫了光輝的詩篇“三吏”和“三别”，表達了對老百姓的深切同情。

在古代史書《新唐書》裏說杜甫離開華州是因爲當地發生饑饉。不過後人認爲他自覺仕途無望，也是加强他的决心的原因。

七五九年七月，杜甫帶領家人長途跋涉，攀越二千多公尺的高山隴山，來到秦州（在今甘肅省內）。他的從姪杜佐住在秦州。杜甫在那兒只眈了大約四個月，因爲親友們給他的經濟上的支持，以及他自己賣藥所得難以維生，甚至他窮得空囊裏只有一個銅板。不僅如此，這時他又發了瘧疾。

正在此時，同谷縣縣令來信邀請他去住。他聽人家說那是個好地方，出產薯蕷、冬笋和蜂蜜。可是事實擺在面前的時候，杜甫發現自己是每況愈下。他們一家是克服了千難萬險，奮力走過巉崖間的險巇的山路，穿過熊羆虎豹的嗥叫聲，才在初冬到達了同谷縣。現在，這位大詩人像是一個山上的野人，衣衫襤褸，灰白的長髮遮面，在雪地裏挖掘黃精，並且爲了充飢，“歲拾橡栗

Tonggu in the early winter. Now the great poet appeared to be like a mountain barbarian in his ragged clothes with rugged, long and grey hair, digging sealworts in the snow, and "picking acorns with the monkey-keeper at the close of the year".

Delaying for one month only, the family started another difficult mountain trip to Chengdu (now in Sichuan Province).

"For three years I tramped among wild mountains with an empty stomach." thus Tu Fu related. In his life journey, this period was the decline in his ambition and livelihood, but the summit of his creative energy with hundreds of excellent poems.

Over hill and dale they came to Chengdu in the dead of winter. The city where Emperor Xuanzong had once taken refuge, was thought a rich, populous and secure harbour.

Tu Fu then began another stage in his life and it was his last ten years.

In the spring of 760, with the financial aid of his cousin Wan Shiwu, the subprefect there, Tu Fu opened up a wasteland and built a thatched cottage in the suburb several miles west of the city, by the Bloom Swimming Brook, on the west side of the Far Reaching Bridge. The cottage was under a tall nanmu tree of about two hundred years old. The area

隨狙公”。

這一家人在同谷只耽了一個月，便開始了另一次艱難的山路旅行到成都（在現在的四川省）。

“三年饑走荒山道”，杜甫這樣自述。這一時期，在他生命的旅程上是他的雄心和生活的下坡路，却是他創作的另一個高峯，其寫出了幾百首精彩的詩篇。

他們翻山越嶺，在隆冬時候來到成都。玄宗曾經在這城裏避難，是一個富庶、繁榮和安全的避居處。

於是，杜甫開始了他生命的另一階段，這是他最後的十年。

七六〇年的春天，杜甫在他的表弟王十五司馬的資助下，開闢了一塊荒地，建築了一座茅屋。地點在成都西郊數里的浣花溪畔，萬里橋西邊。茅屋修建在一株約有二百歲的高大柟樹下。園子起初是一畝地大，在三年的經營之後，大大擴展。他在園子裏種上了桃、李、松、竹、榿、柳、枇杷，各種草藥和花卉。這是鳥雀、水鳥、

of the garden was about one-sixth of an acre at the beginning, and then was extended after three years' labour. He planted in the garden peaches, plums, pines, bamboos, alders, willows, loquats, herbs and many flowers. It was a paradise for Tu Fu, his wife and sons, as well as for birds, aquatic birds, wild fowls, poultry and insects.

For about four years at one time or another Tu Fu lived in the Chengdu Cottage. It was a serene spring after a severe winter; it was an easeful pastoral life after a fury storm. Tu Fu enjoyed the scenery, tilled the land, talked with his neighbours, received visitors of the officialdom and friends, drank wine and wrote poems. Some two hundred and forty of them were written there, such as "My Cottage", "Nine Versicles Written on Impulse", "Rain in a Spring Night" and "The Thatching was Gone with the Autumn Winds" etc.

The Chengdu Cottage, or Tu Fu Cottage, was neglected and ruined after Tu Fu's death until a hundred years later when it was rebuilt by Wei Zhuang (836? – 910), a poet and Prime Minister of the last period of the reign of the Tang Dynasty. Henceforth till now the place has been looked upon as a sacred site.

In the winter of 761, Tu Fu's old friend Gao Shi was appointed acting Prefect of Chengdu for two months; his successor Yan Wu, also a good friend of Tu Fu, had been demoted to the province because of complication in Fang

野禽、家禽和昆蟲的天堂，同時也是杜甫以及他妻子和孩子們的天堂。

杜甫在這成都草堂裏居住前後相加共約四年。這是嚴冬過後明媚的春天；暴風雨過後舒適的田園音樂。他欣賞着美景，耕種着土地，與鄰居們交談，接待着來訪的官員們和朋友們，飲酒賦詩。在那兒寫了二百四十多首。比如：《田舍》、《絕句漫興九首》、《春夜喜雨》和《茅屋爲秋風所破歌》等等。

成都草堂，或稱杜甫草堂，在杜甫死後一直荒蕪着，直到一百年以後，才由唐朝末年的詩人和宰相韋莊（836？——910）重建起來。從那時起直到今天，這個地方被視爲聖地。

七六一年的冬天，杜甫的老友高適奉派暫代成都尹，做了二個月。他的繼任者嚴武也是杜甫的老友，在杜甫被謫遷到華州的時候，他也因牽涉到房琯一案謫遷到蜀地來。他們在遙遠的西部重又會見，欣喜逾常。

Guan's case in which Tu Fu was demoted to Huazhou. Their meeting at the remote west was a very happy occasion.

In 762, Emperor Xuanzong and his son Suzong died in succession, and when Daizong ascended the throne he recalled Yan Wu back to the capital in the Seventh Moon.

Sending Yan Wu off, Tu Fu accompanied him to Mianzhou, and they parted at the Courier Station of Feng Ji. But an accident prevented Tu Fu from going back to his cottage. When the subprefect of Chengdu Xu Zhidao, taking advantage of the absence of Yan Wu, snatched for himself all the official titles that really belonged to Yan Wu, he expanded his territory by armed force. The incident was put down by Gao Shi within a month, but it aroused a great chaos among the people.

In the late autumn of 762 Tu Fu brought his wife from Chengdu to Zizhou. In the Ninth Moon of the next year, Tu Fu hurried alone to Langzhou when he heard that Fang Guan had died there on his way back to the capital. Tu Fu held a memorial ceremony for Fang Guan and wrote a mourning article in deep grief. In the spring of 764, Tu Fu again brought his wife to Langzhou. He had longed for a somewhat important official post in the capital, but Emperor Dai Zong offered him, at this juncture, only the Censorship in General Affairs Department. He refused and decided to boat from Langzhou eastward along the Lang River, Jialing River and Yangtze to Jiangnan, the Land South of the Yangtze.

可是七六二年，玄宗和肅宗父子相繼駕崩，代宗即位的時候，在這年七月召嚴武回長安。

杜甫陪送嚴武到綿州，在奉濟驛分手。一件意外事件阻止了杜甫回到他的草堂。那是成都少尹兼侍御史徐知道，趁嚴武離任之機，把嚴武所有的官銜都加在自己身上，並且派兵擴張地盤。這一事變在一個月之內便被高適平定，但是却給人民帶來了一場大混亂。

七六二年晚秋，杜甫攜妻自成都赴梓州。第二年九月，他聽到房琯在回長安的途中病死於閬州，便隻身奔往該地。他祭了房琯，寫了一篇沉痛的祭文。七六四年的春天，杜甫又攜妻去閬州。他曾經希望在首都得到一個較爲重要的官職，可是這時，代宗只給他一個京兆府功曹參軍的小官。他辭謝不就，決定買棹東下，從閬州沿閬水、嘉陵江、長江，到江南去生活。然而，在最後一刻，一個意料之外的消息使他改變了主意。嚴武重又被任命爲成都尹，並且兼劍南節度使，統管數十州郡。他邀請杜甫往成都，杜甫立刻帶了家小回到他久別的草堂。由於嚴武的舉薦，杜甫被任命爲節度使署中的參謀、檢校工部員外郎，御賜緋魚袋。這種袋是放一種魚形的

And yet an unexpected news changed his mind at the last minute. Yan Wu was commissioned to Chengdu again to be prefect and governor of scores of counties there. He invited Tu Fu to come with him and Tu Fu returned instantly with his family to his long-parted cottage. On Yan Wu's recommendation too, Tu Fu was appointed Staff Officer and Councillor of the Ministry of Works, and awarded by the emperor with a Crimson Fish Bag, which used to contain a fish-shaped credential tally made of gold or silver or bronze. It was a medal symbolizing power and honour, bestowed only on the fifth ranking official and above.

As an official, Tu Fu had to leave his cottage and live in the yamen in the city. The life there was strict and busy, and the personnel matters were complicated as the colleagues, being jealous of Tu Fu's situation, assailed him. Now a man of fifty three, he thought himself old and weak. He had suffered from an illness in lungs and contracted malaria; at this time rheumatism and diabetes came on in quick succession too. The inspissated gloom of his heart we can still feel from the lines of his poem then written, "Lodging in the Yamen".

Once and again Tu Fu wrote poems to Yan Wu, asking for permission to resign. It was not accepted till the third day of the new year of 765. He sought to live a secluded hermit life again in his cottage, but the happy life did not last long for another mishap took place. Yan Wu died in the

符，符用金或銀或銅製成，只賜給五品以上的高官。

作爲一名官吏，杜甫不得不離開草堂，住在城裏的衙門中。幕府的生活嚴格而又忙碌，同時人事關係複雜，幕僚們嫉妒杜甫的地位，不時攻擊他。這時，這位五十三歲的人，感到自己年老體弱，心力交瘁。他曾經患過肺病和瘧疾，此時風痹和消渴症又相繼襲來。他充滿憂鬱的心情我們仍然可以從他這時寫下的《宿府》的詩句中感到。

杜甫一再寫詩給嚴武，要求准許他辭去職務。這一請求直到七六五年正月初三才被接受了。他打算回到草堂重新過那種隱居的生活，可是這種賞心悅目的日子沒有過多久，另一件不幸的事發生了。嚴武在這年四月去世。杜甫在這裏沒有誰可以依靠，也沒有什麼值得依戀

Fourth Moon of the year. Tu Fu had then no one to rely on and nothing to cling to in the place.

In the Fifth Moon of 765, a boat carried Tu Fu and his family cruising down the river. "What I am like that is everywhere wandering? A gull between heaven and earth hovering." he sang in the poem "Reflections in a Night While Travelling".

In autumn, a fit of his chronic illness compelled them to sojourn in Yun-an, a county west of Kuizhou, till the next spring. After that they started to Kuizhou, a mountain county near the Three Gorges, where they lived for one year and nine months. Through the aid of Governor Bai Maolin, Tu Fu had a cosy time there. He borrowed a farmland in the East Field, received a donation of a farm of mandarin orange trees west of the West Stream. He had cottages in both farms and servants to work in the house and farms as well. His sons Tu Zongwen and Tu Zongwu were with him and were helpful.

In his declining years, Tu Fu was now an old invalid with hemiplegia of his right arm, deafness in his left ear, weakness of eyesight, loss of half of his teeth and handicap in walking. In spite of all these, he wrote diligently as ever, and more than four hundred and thirty poems were composed within two years. They are "Reflections in the Autumn, Eight Stanzas", "Night in a Chamber", "Mounting" and "Looking at the Sword Dance performed by the Pupil of the Elder Sister

的了。

七六五年五月，一條木船載着杜甫一家沿江而下。“飄飄何所似？天地一沙鷗。”他在《旅夜書懷》一詩中這樣唱道。

到了秋天，他舊病復發，迫使他們逗留在夔州以西的雲安縣，直到第二年春天。然後啟程往靠近三峽的山城夔州，在這裏住了一年零九個月。受到當地的都督柏茂琳的照顧，杜甫過了一段舒適的日子。他在東屯租了一些公田；柏茂琳又贈送給他在西瀼溪以西的一片柑樹林。在這兩處農莊裏都有他的草堂，還有僕役相幫料理家務和農活。他的兩個兒子宗文和宗武在身邊也能出力。

現在已是杜甫的晚年了。他已是老弱病殘集於一身：他右臂偏枯，左耳失聰，老眼昏花，齒牙落了一半，而且步履艱難。可是儘管如此，他仍然勤奮地寫作，在二年之內完成了四百三十多首詩。例如：《秋興八首》、《閣夜》、《登高》和《觀公孫大娘弟子舞劍器行》等等，等等。

of Kungsun" etc. etc.

Like the odd wild goose attached to its old folk, Tu Fu could not desist from going eastward, and in Kuizhou, the mountainous country, the weather was unhealthy, and the life was isolated. When his younger brother Tu Guan persuaded him by letters to go to him in Jingzhou, Tu Fu led his family starting their migration once more.

It was the beginning of 768, when they boated at Baidi (The White Emperor) City, sailing through the magnificent Three Gorges: Qutang, Wu and Xiling. It was the end of the chapter of his living in Sichuan Province, and the beginning of his last journey.

In the Third Moon they came to Jingzhou of Hubei Province. The place had once been called the South Capital, and was prosperous. One knows not why that Tu Fu mentioned not his brother Tu Guan any more, but lived for a time with his cousin Tu Wei, an official in the city. Old and invalid as he was, Tu Fu met with a tepid reception. The officials treated him with dark eyes, and he was in such a pitiful state that "Bitterly I wag my tail for food".

He could no longer stay there, but where would he go, the homeless, poor, old man in the vast world? As the Tibetans were invading the Central Plains at that time, he could not go northward to Chang-an. He moved at last to Gong-an in

像一隻失羣的孤雁念念不忘牠的故交一樣，杜甫不能忘情於東下；同時夔州這地方山巒重疊，氣候不利於健康，生活又很閉塞。因此，他的弟弟杜觀一再寫信勸他到他所在的荊州的時候，杜甫率領家人開始了又一次的遷徙。

七六八年的正月中旬，他們從白帝城上船，航過壯麗雄偉的瞿塘峽、巫峽和西陵峽。這是杜甫在蜀地生活的終結，也是他最後一段旅程的開始。

是年三月，他們到了荊州（今湖北省江陵縣）。荊州是繁榮的城市，曾一度被稱爲南都。不知爲甚麼杜甫沒有再提到他的弟弟杜觀，却在從弟杜位處住了一個時期。杜位在節度使署任行軍司馬。杜甫老態龍鍾，病體難支，受到冷遇。一些官僚們白眼相看，他窮愁潦倒，甚至“苦搖求食尾”！

此處不能再躭下去了；可是在這茫茫的世界上，這位無家可歸的貧窮的老人能到哪兒去呢？此時，吐蕃正在中原作亂，杜甫無法北上長安，終於在秋末暫遷南邊的公安縣。可是公安縣也發生了變亂，使他不得安身。

the late autumn, but an upheaval broke out giving him no peace too. Again he led his troop in a boat, wandering to Yuezhou, Hengzhou and arrived Tanzhou, Hunan Province, in the late summer of 769.

Here Tu Fu lived like a boatman. The boat was his little floating house. He planted vegetables on the shore and set up a herb stall in the fish market to earn a living. He came across the famous musician and singer Li Guinian. They were both on the downhill in a narrow corner of the world.

In the Fourth Moon of 770, in Tanzhou, General Zang Jie mutinied and killed the Governor, and in the tumult Tu Fu escaped by boat, and returned to Hengzhou.

Now like a piece of leaf tossed up and down in the vastness of the sea, the homeless and aimless boat waved on the waves.

He went upstream along the Chen River, attempting to go to Chenzhou to find his uncle Cui Wei, a censor there. But the swelling flood prevented him and the boat had to moor by the nearby Fangtian Courier Station, Leiyang County. Nie the Prefect, hearing that Tu Fu had come and was detained by the water for five days without anything to eat, sent him plenty of wine and beef. In return, Tu Fu wrote a poem expressing his gratitude. As the flood did not subside, Tu Fu could not but turn the prow northward, prepared to go to Hanyang, and then to Chang-an along the Han River.

他便又帶領他的一隊人乘船飄泊到岳州、衡州，於七六九年的夏末抵達潭州（在今湖南省）。

杜甫在潭州像是一個船民那樣生活。船就是他小小的飄蕩的家。他在岸邊種菜，在漁市上設攤賣藥，以此維生。他遇見了著名的音樂家和歌手李龜年，他們同是天涯淪落人。

七七○年的四月，湖南兵馬使臧玠發動叛變，殺死了潭州刺史崔瓘。在一片混亂中，杜甫乘船逃走，又回到衡州來。

於是，這條沒有家也沒有目標的船顛簸在波濤之中，好像一片樹葉那樣在大海中起伏不定。

他溯着郴水航行，打算到郴州去投靠他在那兒任錄事參軍的舅父崔偉。不料江水大漲，使他不得不停靠在附近的耒陽縣方田驛。耒陽縣令姓聶，聽到杜甫來了，被大水所困，五天都得不到食物，就送了豐盛的白酒和牛肉。杜甫寫了一首感謝的詩作答。洪水滯留不退，杜甫只得掉頭北上，準備去漢陽，然後沿漢水到長安。

But he never reached his destination as poverty, hunger and disease gnawed him and he lay feebler and feebler in the boat floating up-stream on the Xiang River. Before the rest of his familv Tu Fu gasped away his life in the winter of 770, in his fifty ninth winter.

Born a poet, Tu Fu wrote from his youth till his last days, in smooth and rough times alike, though rewardless. It was said he had written about six thousand poems, but now we can only find some one thousand and four hundred. Arranged in order, the poems constitute an autobiography and a chronicle of his time. Thus his works may be called a poetical history.

Born a man of misfortune, he was poor and humble most part of his life, and neglected even by the poetic circles for many many years. There are left to us ten copies of the collected poems of the Tang Dynasty selected by the Tang officials or poets, containing thousand of poems by hundreds of poets, but none except one copy contained Tu Fu's seven poems. The book "More Gems", edited by the poet Wei Zhuang (mentioned above), was printed about a hundred years later after Tu Fu's death.

Born a broad-minded man, Tu Fu always cherished in him the fate of his people, his country and all the things on earth. This, with his incomparable artistry, imparts to his work a tinge of universality and immortality, and we are grateful,

然而他永遠沒有到達這一目的地，因爲貧窮、飢餓和疾病折磨着他，他躺在這條溯湘江北上的小船裏，越來越虛弱了。終於在他家人面前，杜甫在七七〇年的冬天，五十九歲的時候，咽下了最後一口氣。

杜甫天生是一位詩人，他從青年時代直到最後的日子，不論處於順境還是逆境，儘管毫無酬報，他不停地寫着。據說他一共寫了大約六千首詩，然而我們現在只能看到一千四百多首，不過這也是不小的數目了。把他的詩按照先後次序羅列起來，就是他的一篇自傳，也是他的時代的編年史。因此，他的作品可以被人稱做“詩史”。

杜甫天生是一位不幸的人，他的大半生都是貧窮和卑微的，甚至於被詩壇忽視了許多許多年。唐朝的官吏或詩人編選的詩集，我們可以看到有十種，包含上百名詩人的上千首詩，可是其中只有一種選了杜甫的七首詩。那是在杜甫逝世大約一百年以後由詩人韋莊（上面提到過）編印的《又玄集》。

杜甫天生是襟懷寬廣的人，他心中時刻關懷着他的同胞和國家的命運，關懷着世上的一切事物。這一點，再加上他的無可比擬的藝術手腕，使他的作品具有普遍的和不朽的光彩，即使在他去世的一千二百零十周年以

even one thousand two hundred and ten years after his death, for his gift that now belongs to the whole world.

Wu Juntao

June, 16, 1980. Shanghai

後的今天，我們仍然感謝他的這份現在已經屬於全世界的禮物。

吳鈞陶

1980年6月16日　上海

Looking at the Mountain Tai

How should I take the grandiose Mountain Tai?
'Tween Qi and Lu's border the green ranges lie.[1]
The Creator bestows all beauties on,
Its peaks screen daylight and cast shadows long.
The rolls of clouds would lave my bosom on high,
The home-coming birds would lure my staring eye.
Thus I'll ascend to the sky-reaching tops,
And see the mountains around are but dots.

---

[1] Qi (齊) and Lu (魯) were two Kingdoms of ancient China.

望　嶽

岱宗夫如何，
齊魯青未了。
造化鍾神秀，
陰陽割昏曉。
盪胸生曾雲，
決眥入歸鳥。
會當凌絕頂，
一覽衆山小。

Inscribing for Zhang's Recess, Two Stanzas

I

I come alone to your lonely recess in the spring hill;
The chopping of woods echoes in the valley more still.
There remains icy breath in the glen-brooklet after snow;
The sunlights slant through the cliffs, bathing the holt in the glow.
You take no heed of the night aura of gold and silver hoard,
Far from bothers, at dawn, you feast your eyes on the deers' world.
I'm pleased in these all, but devious on the way back,
I'm like an unmoored boat, running off into your track.

II

Nevertheless we meet now and again,
Me in the evening you entertain.
In the clear pond the splashing carp makes a rout,
On the spring lawns the elks and deers bleat out.
The Tu wine that you urge me to drink more;
The pears you need not purchase from outdoor.
The mountain path back of my hamlet is steep,
But I'll not be afraid when I'm drunk deep.

題張氏隱居 二首

一

春山無伴獨相求，
伐木丁丁聲更幽。
澗道餘寒歷冰雪，
石門斜日到林丘。

不貪夜識金銀氣，
遠害朝看麋鹿遊。

乘興杳然迷出處，
對君疑是泛虛舟。

二

之子時相見，
邀人晚興留。
霽潭鱣發發，
春草鹿呦呦。
杜酒偏勞勸，
張梨不外求。
前村山路險，
歸醉每無愁。

The Painting of an Eagle

A whirlwind comes from the scroll of white silk ——
The eagle is a marvel of the painting bilk!
Seeming to hawk at the sly hare, its wings shrug,
And scowling askew, it's all monkey's mug.
One may untie the lustrous jess from the perch,
And beckon it to jump down from the porch.
Why shouldn't it pounce on the wild birds in the sky,
And make their blood drip on earth and feathers fly!

畫鷹

素練風霜起，
蒼鷹畫作殊。
攫身思狡兔，
側目似愁胡。
絛鏇光堪擿，
軒楹勢可呼。
何當擊凡鳥，
毛血洒平蕪。

Evening Feast at Zuo's Manor

Towards the windy trees the slim new moon has set,
Tuning her heart, the lute player's robe with dews is wet.
The dark stream babbles through the blooming banks with
damps,
The spring stars light up the cot, vying with the lamps.
Candles burn short, as we feast our eyes on rare books,
And drink deep, admiring the sword so splendid, it looks.
After rhyming, wafts to ears the Wu dialect song,
Which brings me back to boating there someday bygone.

夜宴左氏庄

風林纖月落。
衣露淨琴張。
暗水流花徑，

春星帶草堂。
檢書燒燭短，
看劍引杯長。
詩罷聞吳咏，
扁舟意不忘。

The Chariots Rattle on

The chariots rattle on, the battle horses neigh;
The footmen each bears bow and arrows by his waist.
Dragging along, their kins have parting words to say,
The Xianyang Bridge's lost in clouds of dust they raised.
Stamping their feet, grasping the clothes, getting in the way,
They cry, their uproars soar up e'en to the clouds grey.

A passer-by asks aside one of the footmen.
"Enlistment is so frequent," thus but states the man.
"At fifteen I was sent north the River to defend,
"Now at forty still I've to go west to till the land.
"The Chief of Hundred wrapp'd my head when first I went,
"Being back with hair grey, yet to far frontier I'm sent.
"A flood of blood is flowing o'er the boundary,
"Emperor Wu still wills extending territory.

"Don't you know, in two hundred counties, east of our country,
"All villages're o'errun with thorns, and all in misery?
"Although there're strong women taking up husbandry,
"Crops in the fields are ploughed disorderly.
"Since soldiers from Chin fight always desperately,
"Like dogs and chickens we're driven to battle-array.

兵車行

車轔轔，馬蕭蕭，
行人弓箭各在腰。
爺娘妻子走相送，
塵埃不見咸陽橋。
牽衣頓足攔道哭，
哭聲直上干雲霄。

道傍過者問行人，
行人但云點行頻。
或從十五北防河，
便至四十西營田。
去時里正與裹頭，
歸來頭白還戍邊。
邊庭流血成海水，
武皇開邊意未已！

君不聞漢家山東二百州，

千村萬落生荊杞。
縱有健婦把鋤犁，
禾生隴畝無東西。
況復秦兵耐苦戰，
被驅不異犬與雞。

"You have the heart to ask me, you venerable man,
"Yet, how can I, a footman, dare to you complain?
"So to say this winter, as by yourself you see,
"They do not let us from the west of the Pass live in peace.[1]
"The County Magistrate duns for the land taxes,
"And by what means can we pay out such and such fees?
"Now really I believe in what the people say:
"To bear a daughter is far better than a son.
"A daughter may marry a next-door neighbour some day,
"A son is fated among wild weeds to lie slain.
"Don't you see, far away at the Lake of Chinhai,
"E'er since the ancient times skulls're spread under the sky?
"The new ghosts are resentful while the old ones cry,
"In the gloomy wet days they sadly wail and sigh!"

---

[1] "The Pass" refers to the Hangu Pass (函谷關). The place west of the Pass was called Chin (秦).

長者雖有問，
役夫敢申恨。
且如今年冬，
未休關西卒。
縣官急索租，
租稅從何出？
信知生男惡，
反是生女好；
生女猶得嫁比鄰，
生男埋沒隨百草。
君不見青海頭，
古來白骨無人收。
新鬼煩冤舊鬼哭，
天陰雨濕聲啾啾。

The Moonlit Night

The moon to-night in Fuzhou's sky,
In chamber you alone will see it floating by.
I'm sorry for our children dear,
As knowing not to yearn for me in Chang-an here.
Your balmy curls are dewy dreams.
Your arms are smooth like jade and chill in lucid beams.
When we'll lean by the gauzy veils,
Both we'll be shone, and then our tears but the dry trails.

雪華
利棣寫

月　夜

今夜鄜州月，
閨中只獨看。
遙憐小兒女，
未解憶長安。
香霧雲鬟濕，
清輝玉臂寒。
何時倚虛幌，
雙照淚痕乾。

Gazing at the Snow

There're e'en more new ghosts crying in battle-field,
I, a lonely old man, sigh, with sorrows filled.
The tumbling clouds lay down the e'ening pall,
The scurry snow-flakes dancing with the squall.
No wine in the cup, the gourd dipper I shove,
A seeming fire-glow in the empty stove.
News from several counties the war prevents,
I sit, fingering out in the air my plaints.

對　雪

戰哭多新鬼，
愁吟獨老翁。
亂雲低薄暮，
急雪舞迴風。
瓢棄樽無綠，
爐存火似紅。
數州消息斷，
愁坐正書空。

A Spring View

As ever are hills and rills while the Kingdom crumbles,
When springtime comes over the Capital the grass scrambles.
Blossoms invite my tears as in wild times they bloom,
The flitting birds stir my heart that I'm parted from home.
For three months the beacon fires soar and burn the skies;
A family letter is worth ten thousand gold in price.
I scratch my head, and my grey hair has grown too thin
It seems, to bear the weight of the hair clasp and pin.[1]

---

[1] In ancient China, men wore long hair bound together on the top of head with the clasp and pin.

雪華利祿寫

春　望

國破山河在，
城春草木深。
感時花濺淚，
恨別鳥驚心。
烽火連三月，
家書抵萬金。
白頭搔更短，
渾欲不勝簪。

The Moon

In Kingdom of Heaven the autumn draws near,
The moonlight shedding on the earth how clear.
The Toad into the crystal waters bounds,
The elixir vitae the Hare fore'er pounds.[1]
Yet only sorrows to my heart you bring,
And on my grey hair lay a silvery ring.
As shields and spears are all o'er the great land,
Shine not, pray, on the camps at the western end!

---

[1] Toad and Hare are characters in the moon in Chinese fairy tales.

月

天上秋期近，
人間月影淸。
入河蟾不沒，
搗藥兔長生。
只益丹心苦，
能添白髮明。
干戈知滿地，
休照國西營。

Composing When Drinking Alone

The snuff of the lamp why flickers merrily?
The emerald wine warms me genially.
A roamer always, I fuddle days away;
My poetic pen a Spirit seems to sway.
In mine eyes soldiers shuttle to and fro;
Confucianism improves my state —— I doubt it's true.
Bound by the low official post, this I dree,
And I feel ashamed toward the people free.

獨酌成詩

燈花何太喜，
酒綠正相親。
醉裏從爲客，
詩成覺有神。
兵戈猶在眼，
儒術豈謀身。
苦被微官縛，
低頭愧野人。

The Jasper Flower Palace

The brook meanders while the winds moan through the pines;
The black rats scrape the ancient tiles in lines.
Who is the Emperor who had built the palace
And left it ruined at the foot of the precipice?
The fatuous fires drift and flicker in the bleak room;
By the destroyed path the rapid waters groan.
All nature's sounds are like the music from reed pipes,
The autumnal scene with its tints is pure and ripe.
A beauty buried had become the yellow loess,
Not to speak of the figures of maids lying in poise.[1]
The guard then guarded the imperial carriage;
A stone horse is only the relic of the stage.
I sit down on the grass and my heart bears a load;
A handful of tears trickle down when I sing a threnode.
Slowly doddering along the human's journey,
Whoever has had immortal longevity?

---

[1] In ancient China there used to be a custom of burying human figures made of wood or earth together with the dead in the tomb.

玉華宮

溪迴松風長，
蒼鼠竄古瓦。
不知何王殿，
遺構絕壁下。
陰房鬼火青，
壞道哀湍瀉。
萬籟眞笙竽，
秋色正蕭灑。
美人爲黃土，
況乃粉黛假。
當時侍金輿，
故物獨石馬。
憂來藉草坐，
浩歌淚盈把。
冉冉征途間，
誰是長年者。

The Winding River, Two Stanzas

I

The whirling of falling petals make the spring pale,
The myriad coloured dots in winds bore me and ail.
Enjoy the flowers are they fade under your eyes,
Don't mind if it's too much but wet your lips with wines.
The kingfishers nest in the river pavilion;
Lies broken by the Park the stone tomb-unicorn.[1]
Nature's law tells us to make life a happy game,
Why should I be bound by the vanity of fame?

II

Everyday after the audience of Court I pawn,[2]
And back from the strand drunk at the cost of my spring gown.

---

[1] The Lotus Park (芙蓉苑) by the Winding River was a famous resort in the Tang dynasty. The sculptured stone unicorns and its kind were usually seated along the path leading to the tomb of the nobleman.

[2] In A.D. 757 - 758, Tu Fu was appointed to be a low official, the Left Censor (左拾遺), and, according to the rule, went to the Imperial Court to attend the audience given by the emperor every early morning.

曲江 二首

其　一

一片花飛減却春，
風飄萬點正愁人。
且看欲盡花經眼，
莫厭傷多酒入唇。
江上小堂巢翡翠，
苑邊高塚臥麒麟。
細推物理須行樂，
何用浮名絆此身。

其　二

朝回日日典春衣，
每日江頭盡醉歸。

At every turn the bills of wine I owed,
Few people lived to be seventy, from of old.
Butterflies perforate the flowers in deep clusters;
Dragonflies skip slow over the surface of waters.
Go round, I say, with scenery so fine, and mind,
Enjoy it for the while, and do not lag behind.

酒債尋常行處有，
人生七十古來稀。
穿花蛺蝶深深見，
點水蜻蜓款款飛。
傳與風光共流轉，
暫時相賞莫相違。

Standing Alone

A vulture hovers about the blue vault of heaven;
Two white gulls float on the rill —— a peaceful haven.
The talons may glide round or swoop down as they please,
While the innocent pair swim to and fro with ease.
The grass moistened with dews is tangling wet;
The spider waiting for preys yet sits in its net.
The dædal Nature is something like human affairs;
Standing alone, a lot of cares my whole heart bears.

獨　立

空外一鷙鳥，
河間雙白鷗。
飄颻搏擊便，
容易往來遊。
草露亦多濕，
蛛絲仍未收。
天機近人事，
獨立萬端憂。

To Hermit Wei, The VIIIth Among His Brothers

How rarely in life we meet together;
Orion and Scorpion too, miss each other.
Ah, what a happy night it is to-night;
We sit, face to face, in the candle light!
How many days one can claim young and sound?
On our temples much grey hair can be found.
Half of our friends have given up the ghost,
I cry, when I visit them, my bowels roast.
I never expected twenty years have fled
Before I come again to your homestead.
You were unmarried the day I left erstwhile,
Your sons and daughters now stand in a file.
They gladly greet their father's bosom friend,
And ask me if I've come from a strange land.
We are busy in our conversation
While wine and all are in preparation.
The leeks are cut in the spring night, raining,
The meal with yellow millet is hot steaming.
My host says it is very hard to meet,
Raising for ten times his goblet to greet.
It does not make me drunk even quaffing ten,
Owing to my grateful heart can I sustain.
Tomorrow, betwixt us the mountain will intrude.
We'll each be lost in the vastness of the world!

贈衛八處士

人生不相見，
動如參與商。
今夕復何夕，
共此燈燭光。
少壯能幾時，
鬢髮各已蒼。
訪舊半爲鬼，
驚呼熱中腸。
焉知二十載，
重上君子堂。
昔別君未婚，
兒女忽成行。
怡然敬父執，
問我來何方。
問答乃未已，
兒女羅酒漿。
夜雨剪春韮，
新炊間黃粱。
主稱會面難，
一舉累十觴。
十觴亦不醉，
感子故意長。
明日隔山岳，
世事兩茫茫。

The Official of Xin-an County[1]

I travel on the Xin-an Pavement,
I hear the noisy call of enlistment.
To my query, answers the county prefect —
"We've no more adult in our little tract,
"And last night came down the army bulletins,
"Now only to conscribe boys out of teens."
The teen-agers are very greeny and short,
How can they defend the Emperor's fort?
The bonny ones have mothers seeing them off,
While the boys thin and bony are kept aloof.
The pale waters ripple eastward at eve,
The echoes of cries yet in green mountains live.

---

[1] There is a group of poems of Tu Fu known as "Three Officials" and "Three Partings", consisting of "The Official of Xin-an County", "The Official of Tong Pass", "The Officials of Stone-Ditch Village", "Parting of the Newly Married Pair", "Parting of the Old Couple" and "Parting of the Homeless Man".
Tu Fu wrote these poems in the year. A.D. 759, when Governor An Lushan (安祿山) and Shi Siming (史思明) rebelled against the Tang dynasty. Premier Guo Ziyi (郭子儀) and other governors fought them at Ye City (鄴城), but lost the battle. The government was badly frightened at the situation and searched rudely everywhere for more people to serve in the army. Tu Fu, in a contradictory state of mind – sympathetic with the people, and abhorring the rebels at the same time – wrote down the famous six poems.

新安吏

客行新安道，
喧呼聞點兵。
“借問新安吏：
縣小更無丁？”
“府帖昨夜下，
次選中男行。”
“中男絕短小，
何以守王城？”
肥男有母送，
瘦男獨伶俜。
白水暮東流，
青山猶哭聲！

Oh, country men, please don't weep your eyes dry,
And hold in your dripping tears, please don't cry.
Heaven and Earth are ever cruel and dull,
E'en though your eyes are drained on a skull!
Our troops have the Ye City besieged,
We hoped night and day it'll be seized.
Yet the foes were incalculably cunning,
Our camps scattered about, like stars running.
Troops drew back, near the old base, for provisions,
And in Luoyang, drilled for preparations.
Recruits will trench, but not deeply to the water,
Or graze horses there, also an easy matter.
Moreo'er, our Emperor's troops are regal,
Your sons will be tended and treated well.
Don't weep tears of blood when parting with them here,
The Premier is like father and brother dear!

“莫自使眼枯，
收汝淚縱橫！
眼枯即見骨，
天地終無情！
我軍取相州，
日夕望其平。
豈意賊難料，
歸軍星散營。
就糧近故壘，
練卒依舊京。
掘壕不到水，
牧馬役亦輕。
況乃王師順，
撫養甚分明。
送行勿泣血，
僕射如父兄。”

The Official of Tong Pass

How weary are the privates in their toil
O'er building walls, at Tong Pass, with the soil.
The towers here and there, bigger and smaller,
Are iron-bound, ten thousand feet, and taller.
I ask the official of Tong Pass, and he describes,
"Once more, it's to guard against Northern Tribes."
Inviting me to dismount and have a walk
With him, he points about their mountain work.
"The palisades thrust high to clouds in the sky;
"Birds e'en can't manage over them to fly.
"We need but hold the place if the tribes invade,
"And Chang-an would be kept out of their raid.
"Please, sir, look at the vital place, so narrow
"That it allows but one chariot to go through.
"E'er since ancient times when began the war,
"One lancer's enough to guard the strait door.
"Woe has been the battle at Peach Trees Fort,
"Millions of soldiers died like fish of a sort.
"Please tell the Pass Commandant to be discreet,
"Not like Geshu Han who suffered a defeat."[1]

---

[1] In the Sixth Moon, A.D. 756, Geshu Han (哥舒翰), a general in the Tang dynasty, leading an army of two hundred thousand soldiers, fought against the rebellious army at Peach Trees Fort

潼關吏

士卒何草草，
築城潼關道。
大城鐵不如，
小城萬丈餘。
借問潼關吏，
修關還備胡！
要我下馬行，
爲我指山隅：
連雲列戰格，
飛鳥不能逾。
胡來但自守；
豈復憂西都！
丈人視要處，
窄狹容單車。
艱難備長戟，
萬古用一夫。
哀哉桃林戰，
百萬化爲魚。
請囑防關將：
愼勿學哥舒！

(桃林塞), a district in the suburbs of Tong Pass (潼關). He was badly beaten, and thousands of his soldiers fell and were drowned in the Yellow River in the rout.

The Officials of Stone-Ditch Village

In Stone-Ditch Village, in the eve, I lodge,
At midnight come the seizers while the cotters dodge.
I hear the old man climbing o'er the wall,
His old wife going to answer the call.
How peevishly the cruel officials shout,
How sadly the old wife sobs her heart out!
And hark to her story, what a pity:
"My three sons have gone to guard Ye City.
"One of them recently wrote me a letter,
"Telling that two brothers were killed in a battle.
"The living has his life but for the present,
"The dead ones are fore'er from the world absent!
"In our home there's no man among the rest,
"Except a grandson still sucking at the breast.
"His mother is with us, but can't guest you,
"As she has only a shabby skirt to show.
"I, an old woman, am too weak to fight,
"Still I'd like to go with you, sir, to-night.
"Hurrying on to Heyang for the service,
"I may cook breakfast in time for soldiers."
Her voice fades away as the night deepens,
It seems to linger in the air —— her weepings.
At day-break, further on my way I'd ply,
To the old man alone I bid good-bye.

石壕吏

暮投石壕村，
有吏夜捉人。
老翁逾墻走，
老婦出門看。
吏呼一何怒！
婦啼一何苦！
聽婦前致詞：
三男鄴城戍。
一男附書至，
二男新戰死。
存者且偷生，
死者長已矣！
室中更無人，
惟有乳下孫。
有孫母未去，
出入無完裙。
老嫗力雖衰，
請從吏夜歸。
急應河陽役，
猶得備晨炊。
夜久語聲絕，
如聞泣幽咽。
天明登前途，
獨與老翁別。

Parting of the Newly Married Couple

Attaching to the rushes and hemps in drills,
The dodders cannot draw long their tendrils.
Marrying a daughter for a footman's bride,
One'd better forsake her by the wayside.
I dressed my hair and became your mate,
And in your bed, we didn't e'en warm the mat.
Wasn't it such a hurry that you've taken leave
In the morn, while we married just last eve?
I know that you have not gone far afield,
But to guard the front in Heyang battle-field.
But how I'll treat your parents as of mine?
I'm new-come in the family of thine.
When I was brought up my old folks were tight,
They kept me in my chamber day and night.
And told me whene'er betrothed to someone,
No matter a dog or chicken, it's fore'er done.
And now you have gone to the place of death,
My heart sinks within me and aches in one breath.
I've vowed to go with you anywhere,
But the situation was intense and drear.
Oh, set aside the thinking of our nuptial life,
Do your best in the military strife.
A woman comes with you in the army,

雪華 利祿寫

新婚別

兎絲附蓬麻，
引蔓故不長。
嫁女與征夫，
不如棄路旁。
結髮爲妻子，
席不暖君床。
暮婚晨告別，
無乃太匆忙！
君行雖不遠，
守邊赴河陽。
妾身未分明，
何以拜姑嫜？
父母養我時，
日夜令我藏。
生女有所歸，
鷄狗亦得將。
君今往死地，
沉痛迫中腸！
誓欲隨君去，
形勢反蒼黃！
勿爲新婚念，
努力事戎行！
婦人在軍中，

May possibly make martial spirit barmy.
I come from a poor family and I sigh,
My gauze coat had cost my parents much to buy.
No more shall I wear my best coat brand-new,
I'll wash off powder and rouge —— for you.
I look up to all kinds of birds flying,
Big or small, they are all in pairs gliding.
The human affairs are always wrong and sour,
But I crave for you fore'er with heart and soul!

兵氣恐不揚。
自嗟貧家女，
久致羅襦裳。
羅襦不復施，
對君洗紅妝！
仰視百鳥飛，
大小必雙翔。
人事多錯迕，
與君永相望！

Parting of the Old Couple

Peace comes not to the four corners of the earth,
Old as I am, nowhere to take up a berth.
Sons and grandsons have all in fighting died,
And why should I alone save my own hide?
Throwing away the stick I leave my home;
Companions sympathize with me for my doom.
Fortunately my teeth are good as yet,
Lamentably my marrow in me has set.
As a man, and in armour being clad,
I bow with folded hands to part with the Head.
While lying on the way cries my old mate,
Her dress's too thin, for the year's drawing late.
I know it's a farewell forevermore,
And thinking she may catch cold I feel sore.
I'll ne'er return when I start to leave here,
Her bidding me to take care can I still hear.
The walls of Clay Gate Pass are strongly made,
The Apricot Garden's hard for the foes to invade.
It's different now from Ye City's defeat,
We shall have time to spend ere Death we meet.
There're separations and reunions in life,
When in your dotage like when you look alive.
Recalling the old times when I was young,

垂老別

四郊未寧靜，
垂老不得安。
子孫陣亡盡，
焉用身獨完?!
投杖出門去，
同行爲辛酸。
幸有牙齒存，
所悲骨髓乾。
男兒既介冑，
長揖別上官。
老妻臥路啼，
歲暮衣裳單。
孰知是死別，
且復傷其寒！
此去必不歸，
還聞勸加餐！
土門壁甚堅，
杏園度亦難。
勢異鄴城下，
縱死時猶寬。
人生有離合，
豈擇盛衰端？
憶昔少壯日，

I sink in various thoughts and sigh for long.
All nations are involved in warfare,
The beacon fires roll on hills here and there.
The sanguinary corpses stench the plants,
And blood smears red the rivers and the plains.
Where could be the Land of Happiness?
Why should I stagger still with tardiness?
Renouncing my humble cottage I'll go;
My heart in my chest collapses with woe!

遲回竟長嘆。
萬國盡征戍，
烽火被岡巒。
積屍草木腥，
流血川原丹。
何鄉爲樂土？
安敢尚盤桓！
棄絕蓬室居，
塌然摧肺肝。

Parting of the Homeless Man

Since the rebellion of the Tianbao period, [1]
In wormwoods and pigweeds the farms are buried.
There were a hundred families in our town,
East or west they've fled ere they could settle down.
There is no news from those who are alive,
And dust and mud are those who lost their life.
From the rout of Ye City I come back
To find in my birth place the dear old track.
The empty lanes meet my eyes all the way,
The sun seems to be haggard, the air dreary.
Me the foxes and racoon-dogs do defy,
With their hair standing up, and furiously cry.
What are there in my neighbour's houses all round?
Only one or two widows can be found.
Clinging to their old perch, the tired birds fly,
Shall I leave my poor nest and further ply?
In spring I shoulder a hoe to farm alone,
And water vegetable plots in gloom.
But the official knows I'm back a farmer,

---

[1] Tianbao (天寶) period (A.D. 742 – 755), one of the periods when Emperor Xuanzong (玄宗) reigned in the Tang dynasty. Toward the end of the period began the rebellion of An Lushan (安祿山) and Shi Siming (史思明).

無家别

寂寞天寶後，
園廬但蒿藜！
我里百餘家，
世亂各東西。
存者無消息，
死者爲塵泥。
賤子因陣敗，
歸來尋舊蹊。
久行見空巷，
日瘦氣慘悽。
但對狐與狸，
竪毛怒我啼！
四鄰何所有？
一二老寡妻。
宿鳥戀本枝，
安辭且窮棲？
方春獨荷鋤，
日暮還灌畦。
縣吏知我至，

He calls me to be trained as a drummer!
To serve within the County, it's all very well,
Yet at home I've no one to bid farewell.
All by myself, to a near camp I make way,
I would be the more at sea if far away.
Near or far, it makes no difference to me,
While all's gone in town, but a blank to see.
I'm torn with grief, my mother died of disease
Five years ago, the gutter was her release.
How worthless I was born and live above ground,
My mother and I suffer without bound!
A homeless man to part with his birth place,
What a shame, being one of the human race!

召令習鼓鼙。
雖從本州役，
內顧無所攜。
近行止一身，
遠去終轉迷。
家鄉既蕩盡，
遠近理亦齊！
永痛長病母，
五年委溝溪。
生我不得力，
終身兩酸嘶。
人生無家别，
何以爲蒸黎？

The Surpassing Beauty

There is a surpassing beauty
Who lives in a solitary valley.
She says she comes from a good family,
And now declines into the wild country.
"When riot broke out in the Capital City,
"My brothers were killed in the mutiny.
"High officials they were, but not worthy,
"In fact, e'en to lie in peace under the clay.
"The world always shrinks from vile destiny,
"And hollow is left to me like a candle burning dimly.
"My husband is a light-minded bonny;
"He then married another fair lady.
"When night falls, the mimosa feels sleepy,
"And mandarin-ducks ne'er live separately.
"He sees but his new bride's smiles so merry;
"How could he care for me weeping days away?
"The spring water is limpid in the valley;
"When it flows out of the dale it becomes filthy.
"I've sent my maid to sell pearls for money,
"When she's back, we'll mend our hut with ivy.
"I pluck flowers, but not on my hair display,
"A handful of cypress is often my toy.
"In the cold air my thin green sleeves are wavy,
"In sun-set I lean on the bamboo wearily!"

佳　人

絕代有佳人，
幽居在空谷。
自云良家子，
零落依草木。
關中昔喪亂，
兄弟遭殺戮。
官高何足論？
不得收骨肉。
世情惡衰歇，
萬事隨轉燭。
夫婿輕薄兒，
新人美如玉。
合昏尙知時，
鴛鴦不獨宿。
但見新人笑，
那聞舊人哭！
在山泉水淸，
出山泉水濁。
侍婢賣珠回，
牽蘿補茅屋。
摘花不插髮，
採柏動盈掬。
天寒翠袖薄，
日暮倚修竹。

Dreaming of Li Po, Two Stanzas[1]

I

We sob when Death comes rending us apart,
And parting alive, too, would wrench our heart.
Yon Jiangnan is known as the malarious mire,[2]
No news of you yet come from the exile.
Knowing that how I think of you always,
Into my dreams, so you have made your ways.
But I'm afraid it's not the soul of you old,
Since it's a long way and nothing can be told.
As your soul nears the maple trees that turn blue,
And the frontier is darkened when back you go.
You are now in the meshes of the law,
How can you have wings and elude the paw?
The setting moonlight floods over the beams,
Your features still is lighted up there, it seems.
Deep are the waters, billows widely spread,
Mind, and be sure the dragons wouldn't be fed!

---

[1] Li Po, the great poet and Tu Fu's intimate friend, being involved in a military action led by Prince Li Lin (李璘), was exiled by Emperor Suzong to a remote country Yelang (夜郎) in the year 758. Anxious about Li Po's fate, Tu Fu wrote these poems.

[2] *Jiang* (river) *nan* (south), a general term for the vast territory south of the Yangtze River.

夢李白 二首

其 一

死別已吞聲，
生別常惻惻。
江南瘴癘地，
逐客無消息。
故人入我夢，
明我長相憶。
恐非平生魂，
路遠不可測。
魂來楓林青，
魂返關塞黑。
君今在羅網，
何以有羽翼？
落月滿屋梁，
猶疑照顏色。
水深波浪闊，
無使蛟龍得！

II

The floating clouds are strolling all day long,
You wanderer for a long time have gone.
I dreamt of you three nights repeatedly,
It means you want me too, whole-heartedly.
Whenever leaving you seemed to hesitate,
"It's hard for me to come," you sadly state.
"The way is rough with billows and winds groan,
"The boat may possibly be overthrown."
Out of the door you scratch your hoary hair,
As if fulfil not your will you despair.
High officials are crowded in Chang-an,
You only are neglected, thin and wan.
Who says the network of the Void is vast?
When aging you are caught in the meshes fast!
Your fame will last forever and ever,
Yet then you've lonely past the world over!

其　二

浮雲終日行，
遊子久不至。
三夜頻夢君，
情親見君意。
告歸常局促，
苦道來不易。
江湖多風波，
舟楫恐失墜。
出門搔白首，
若負平生志。
冠蓋滿京華，
斯人獨憔悴。
孰云網恢恢，
將老身反累。
千秋萬歲名，
寂寞身後事！

Thinking of My Brothers in a Moonlit Night

The garrison drums warning the pass to be clear,
A wild goose honks above the autumnal frontier.
The season called the White Dew begins to-night,[1]
Nowhere like in our native place the moon's so bright.
I'm very worried about my brothers' existence,
And no place to ask and connect our far distance.
Letters I sent, but reached them not even a word,
The warfare still is going in the mundane world!

---

[1] According to the traditional Chinese calendar, there are twenty-four divisions in a year. White Dew is the name of one of the divisions, that occurs in September.

月夜憶舍弟

戍鼓斷人行，
邊秋一雁聲。
露從今夜白，
月是故鄉明。
有弟皆分散，
無家問死生。
寄書長不達，
況乃未休兵。

At the End of the World I Think of Li Po

At the end of the world here rises the cold wind,
And how is it like —— the frame of your mind?
When the news of you will be brought me by wild goose?
The journey all along there are autumn pools.
Good fortune always likes not good writings,
While demons hug themselves on man's missings.
Will you talk with the poet that died of despite,
By bestowing a poem on the Milo's tide? [1]

---

[1] Qu Yuan (屈原 , about 340 – 278 B.C.), the poet of the Warring Kingdoms Period (戰國) and a stateman of his country Chu (楚). He was vilified by his colleague, downgraded and exiled. He drowned himself with grudge at last in the Milo River (汨羅江). Poets and scholars of later years wrote poems or articles in memory of him whenever they passed by the river.

天末懷李白

涼風起天末，
君子意如何？
鴻雁幾時到，
江湖秋水多。
文章憎命達，
魑魅喜人過。
應共冤魂語，
投詩贈汨羅。

Impressions

With sullen eyes I see the twinkling dew
On the chrysanthemums blooming in time due.
The chilly winds chase the broken osiers;
The reed-pipe elicits the roamer's tears.
The tower's shadow in the water sleeps;
The mountain pass in the dying sun steeps.
The nestling birds're mute under the night cloak;
Only the late coming crows hardly croak.

遣　懷

愁眼看霜露，
寒城菊自花。
天風隨斷柳，
客淚墮清笳。
水靜樓陰直，
山昏塞日斜。
夜來歸鳥靜，
啼殺後棲鴉。

New Moon

With a thread of light the new moon climbs up the blue;
It's not a round wheel as the shadow looks askew.
The while gleaming above the ancient fort beyond,
She has slunk into the clouds and can hardly be found.
The constellated Milky Way is always bright;
The frontier mountain pass looms upon the chill site.
The crystalline dew-drops scatter in the little park;
The clusters of chrysanthemums glisten in the dark.

初　月

光細弦初上，
影斜輪未安。
微升古塞外，
已隱暮雲端。
河漢不改色，
關山空自寒。
庭前有白露，
暗滿菊花團。

Pounding the Clothes

I know well that you'll not come back from the frontier,
When autumn comes still I wash the washing stone clear.
Because the months severely cold are drawing near,
Still more, I suffer from parting many a year.
Should I be tired in pounding and give up with tear?
Nay, I'll send the clothes afar to the Great Wall to my dear.
Never shall I spare the strength of mine, a female mere,
The echoes resounding the sphere I wish you'll hear.

擣衣

亦知戍不返，
秋至拭清砧。
已近苦寒月，
況經長別心。
寧辭擣衣倦，
一寄塞垣深。
用盡閨中力，
君聽空外音。

The Glowworm

By chance you're born from grasses of decay,
Dare you fly near where shines the light of day?
You're not so bright as to illume the scrolls,
But sometimes spangle the robe of one who strolls.
Veering outside the veils you're small in the wind,
Soaking with rain by woods you have a frail rind.
Frost is heavy when comes the Tenth Moon,
Drifting alone, where then will you roam?

螢　火

幸因腐草出，
敢近太陽飛？
未足臨書卷，
時能點客衣。
隨風隔幔小，
帶雨傍林微。
十月清霜重，
飄零何處歸？

The Autumnal Fluting

How bitter the notes sound again and again,
And drops of blood the player's garment stain!
The other day you will be sad e'en more,
When soldiers are back as skeletons and gore.
We meet, and may regret the time to part,
So you croon the flute with a melting heart.
Can't I see the sorrowing clouds flowing,
But I feel the lamenting winds soughing!

秋 笛

清商欲盡奏，
奏苦血霑衣。
他日傷心極，
征人白骨歸。
相逢恐恨過，
故作發聲微。
不見愁雲動，
悲風稍稍飛。

Ode To My Cottage Unroofed by the Autumn Gales

In the Eighth Moon, the autumn gales howl from on high;
The thrice-laid thatch rolls from my roof to the sky.
Scattered about, across the river, the straws fly,
On the tips of the tall trees they hang and twine,
Or swirling down to the pools they sink and lie.

Urchins from Southern Village tease that I'm an old one,
They rob, under my eyes, in the face of the sun,
By holding armfuls of straws, and actually run
Into the bamboos, taking my shouting as fun.
I can only come back, and leaning on my cane groan.

Meanwhile, the clouds are dark as ink when the gales cease,
And the autumn sky is veiled in dusky sheets.
Cold as iron is the quilt worn for many years;
My boy, sleeping ill, trod the lining into pieces.
Wet is at the bed-side, as the roof there has leaks;
The raindrops drip successively down like hemp seeds.
E'er since the upheaval we've been short of sleeps;
How to endure the soakage till the long night flees?

If there were spacious houses, thousands and more,
Sheltering all the world to the joy of the poor,

茅屋爲秋風所破歌

八月秋高風怒號，
卷我屋上三重茅；
茅飛渡江灑江郊，
高者掛罥長林梢，
下者飄轉沉塘坳。

南村羣童欺我老無力，
忍能對面爲盜賊，
公然抱茅入竹去；
脣焦口燥呼不得，
歸來倚杖自嘆息。

俄頃風定雲墨色，
秋天漠漠向昏黑。
布衾多年冷似鐵，
嬌兒惡臥踏裏裂。
床頭屋漏無乾處，
雨脚如麻未斷絕。
自經喪亂少睡眠，
長夜沾濕何由徹。

安得廣廈千萬間，
大庇天下寒士俱歡顏，

Unshaken like the mountains in the storm's uproar!
Alas! I'd prefer my cot ruins, I myself frozen to death,
To the towering houses that one day stand in my face!

風雨不動安如山。
嗚呼！何時眼前突兀見此屋？
吾廬獨破受凍死亦足！

An Outfield View

The autumnal view is infinite for one's gaze,
And far away somewhere roll up the wreathes of haze.
The river flows to meet the heaven pure and cold,
The lonely city hides itself in fog's deep fold.
Drifting with winds the sparse yellow leaves are gone,
Dipping behind the distant hills the sun is down.
Why are you late, odd crane, in flying back to your nest?
The evening crows have crowded in the forest.

野　望

清秋望不極，
迢遞起層陰。
遠水兼天淨，
孤城隱霧深。
葉稀風更落，
山迥日初沉。
獨鶴歸何晚，
昏鴉已滿林。

The Sick Horse

You give me a ride for many a year,
Now it is cold at the mountain pass here.
Towards the year's end, on the path muddy,
I'm sorry you towing your old, sick body.
Is it special of your bones and sinew?
You're docile and tame ever since I knew.
You're noble-minded, though you look humble,
I sigh, and the waves in my heart tumble.

病　馬

乘爾亦已久，
天寒關塞深。
塵中老盡力，
歲晚病傷心。
毛骨豈殊衆，
馴良猶至今。
物微意不淺，
感動一沉吟。

The Brazen Vase

The well, ruined in wartime, is moss-grown;
The palace, wherein it stands, was a great dome.
The brazen vase was busy then to drink
And draw the pulley groaning at the brink.
There would have been a fair court maid by its side,
Glassed herself in the cold depth and sighed.
The dragon is now half jagged on the mould;
Still the antique vase costs something in gold.

銅 瓶

亂後碧井廢，
時清瑤殿深。
銅瓶未失水，
百丈有哀音。
側想美人意，
應悲寒甃沉。
蛟龍半缺落，
猶得折黃金。

Seeing Someone off Far Away

On heaven and earth there with armoured men swarm,
And what made you go far away with qualm?
Your kith and kin were weeping out their groan,
You were in the saddle to the city lone.
Plants are wilted when it's late in the year;
The Pass and river are frosted with snow clear.
The wrench lasts hard since yesterday you left,
Now I know how our betters' hearts were reft.

送 遠

帶甲滿天地，
胡爲君遠行。
親朋盡一哭，
鞍馬去孤城。
草木歲月晚，
關河霜雪淸。
別離已昨日，
因見古人情。

The Choice of Abode

Tracing up the Bloom Swimming Stream to the west end,
With the quiet trees and pools, the lord finds me a land.
Leaving the city, I leave the secular affairs,
And yet the clear waters would purge my heart from cares.
Up and down, a swarm of dragonflies flutter swift;
Stand and fall, a pair of purple mandarine-ducks drift.
To go thousands of miles eastwards, while the whims last,
Shanyin the resort — a junk can carry me there fast.

卜居

浣花溪水水西頭，
主人爲卜林塘幽。
已知出郭少塵事，
更有澄江銷客憂。
無數蜻蜓齊上下，
一雙鸂鶒對沉浮。
東江萬里堪乘興，
須向山陰上小舟。

The Completion of My Cottage

In the back of the city my reed roofed cottage is built;
By the riverside path it e'er looks on the green field.
The leaves of alders rift the sun and sing in the breeze;
The dews drip down the bamboos' tips with misty wreaths.
The birds with their fledgelings roost there for a rest,
The churring swallows frequent to make a new nest.
Some others mistake to compare here to Yang Xiong's house;[1]
I'm too lazy to write "Excuse" to stop their mouth.

---

[1] Yang Xiong (楊雄 , 53 B.C. — A.D. 18), a scholar of the Han dynasty, had had a house nearby Tu Fu's cottage. "Excuse" was one of his articles.

堂成

背郭堂成蔭白茅，
緣江路熟俯青郊。
榿林礙日吟風葉，
籠竹和烟滴露梢。
暫止飛鳥將數子，
頻來語燕定新巢。
旁人錯比揚雄宅，
懶惰無心作解嘲。

My Cottage

The limpid river winding by my cottage,
The wicket door opens to the old passage.
The ruts to market town are all grass-grown;
Living remote, I mind not my shabby gown.
The willows frailly swing their strings of hair,
The loquats cluster on trees, scenting the air.
The sun is westering with golden rings;
On kiddles the cormorants bask their wings.

雪華利祿画

田　舍

田舍清江曲，
紫門古道旁。
草深迷市井，
地僻懶衣裳。
楊柳枝枝弱，
枇杷樹樹香。
鸕鷀西日照，
曬池滿漁梁。

The Temple of the Prime Minister of Shu[1]

Where to find the deceased Prime Minister's Temple?
Outside Chengdu, under the cypresses' arch ample.
The grass round the steps reflects the colour of spring;
The oriole amid the leaves vainly sings its strain.
Thrice the Emperor to him came for the plan to rule;
For two reigns the noble statesman served heart and soul.[2]
Uncertain of victory, he died in the camp ground,
It oft makes later heroes weep with sighs profound!

---

[1] The Prime Minister of Shu (蜀, now Sichuan Province, 四川省) is Zhuge Liang (諸葛亮 , 181 – 234), the famous statesman and strategist in the period of the Three Kingdoms (三國, 220 – 265): Wei, Shu and Wu (魏、蜀、吳).

[2] Zhuge Liang had served Emperor Liu Bei (劉備 , 161 – 223) and his son Emperor Liu Chan (劉禪 , 207 – 271).

蜀 相

丞相祠堂何處尋？
錦官城外柏森森。
映階碧草自春色，
隔葉黃鸝空好音。
三顧頻煩天下計，
兩朝開濟老臣心。
出師未捷身先死，
長使英雄淚滿襟。

Village by the Riverside

The lucid river swerves and holds the village in arm,
On these long summer days the rural life here is all calm.
Swallows come freely in and out the hall of my cottage,
While gulls snuggle to each other at the water's edge.
Lining a paper chequer my wife bends over her work,
Knocking a needle my son is making a fishing hook.
A martyr of illness, what I want is medicines,
What else should I seek for my humble being than these things?

江　村

清江一曲抱村流，
長夏江村事事幽。
自去自來堂上燕，
相親相近水中鷗。
老妻畫紙爲棋局，
稚子敲針作釣鉤。
多病所須唯藥物，
微軀此外復何求？

Nine Versicles Written on Impulse

I

Seeing that I, a roamer, can't from sorrow recover,
Roguish spring you'd still come to my hut by the river.
It's blundering that you send the flowers blooming;
Too solicitously you set the orioles tuning.

II

I planted the peaches and plums, they can't claim they're free,
Although the courtyard wall is low, it's a home for me.
It seems I, an oldster, am teased by the spring squall:
Last night it made some twigs of flowers break and fall.

III

The swallows know well that my hut is small and low,
So from the river often they come to and fro.
They stain my lute and scrolls when pecking mud for nest,
And flitter over me while chasing the flying pest.

IV

The Third Moon comes as the Second Moon wastes away,
I'm growing old and how many more times can I meet spring
day?

絕句漫興九首

眼見客愁愁不醒，
無賴春色到江亭。
即遣花開深造次，
便教鶯語太丁寧。

手種桃李非無主，
野老牆低還是家。
恰似春風相欺得，
夜來吹折數枝花。

熟知茅齋絕低小，
江上燕子故來頻。
銜泥點污琴書內，
更接飛蟲打著人。

二月已破三月來，
漸老逢春能幾回。

Don't be worrying o'er the endless mortal coil,
But take the horn while you can ere you lie in the soil.

V

Heart-broken, I stroll with a goose-foot stick, and stand,
Near the spring river's source, on the islet, on the sand.
The willow catkins with the wind dance in random,
The peach blossoms that swirl with the current are wanton.

VI

Too indolent to go out of the village,
I call my son to stay and close the door of hedge.
I'm all alone with wine in the quiet mossy bosk,
The spring winds dimple the green water in rural dusk.

VII

The willow catkins pave the path with a white blanket,
The lotus leaves are copper coins on the brooklet.
A fledgeling pheasant hides behind the bamboo shoot,
On the sand-bar young ducks roost by their mam's foot.

VIII

West to my hut, the mulberry leaves are tender,
Along the river, the wheat waves in blades slender.
Spring lengthens into summer, and how long will life last?
Never let the honey-sweet wine go vainly past!

莫思身外無窮事，
且盡生前有限杯。

腸斷春江欲盡頭，
杖藜徐步立芳洲。
顛狂柳絮隨風舞，
輕薄桃花逐水流。

懶慢無堪不出村，
呼兒自在掩柴門。
蒼苔濁酒林中靜，
碧水春風野外昏。

糝徑楊花鋪白氈，
點溪荷葉疊青錢。
筍根雉子無人見，
沙上鳧雛傍母眠。

舍西柔桑葉可拈，
江畔細麥復纖纖。
人生幾何春已夏，
不放香醪如蜜甜。

IX

The willow next-door swings its branches very fine,
Like a maiden of fifteen with her soft waist-line.
Who says that it is not by intention at dawn,
That the violent winds break the longest branches down?

隔戶楊柳弱嫋嫋，
恰似十五女兒腰。
謂誰朝來不作意，
狂風挽斷最長條。

Receiving a Guest

— a Hearty Welcome to Prefect Tsui

To the south and north of my cottage there're spring waters,
The groups of gulls only are my daily visitors.
The floral path hasn't been swept as no one happens
To come, but now for you the wicket door opens.
Far from the market, there's a simple meal to dine,
A needy family, but the home-brewed old wine.
Would you care to drink with my venerable neighbour,
Toasting the last cups, over the fence of bamboo?

客至

喜崔明府相過

舍南舍北皆春水，
但見羣鷗日日來。
花徑不曾緣客掃，
蓬門今始爲君開。
盤飧市遠無兼味，
樽酒家貧只舊醅。
肯與鄰翁相對飲，
隔籬呼取盡餘杯。

Rain in a Spring Night

The favourable rain its season knows,
It drizzles down when Spring her breaths blows.
Diving and melting into night with winds,
It mutely moistens Earth with wary minds.
The clouds and the wild path are very dark,
The only light is from the river bark.
At day-break in Chengdu where is red and wet
There you'll see blooms bow under heavy weight.

春夜喜雨

好雨知時節，
當春乃發生。
隨風潛入夜，
潤物細無聲。
野徑雲俱黑，
江船火獨明。
曉看江濕處，
花重錦官城。

Spring Flood

In March, when the peach blooms, the spring flood swells,
The river is recovering its old trails.
At morn it overflows the sandbank's tails,
While the cottage door is waving in blue swirls.
With jointed strings they dangle about sweet baits,
And spliced bamboo pipes water the small garden beds.
From nowhere there have come down many birds,
Chattering, bickering in their happy bathe.

春　水

三月桃花浪，
江流復舊痕。
朝來沒沙尾，
碧色動柴門。
接縷垂芳餌，
連筒灌小園。
已添無數鳥，
爭浴故相喧。

Sunset

The setting sunlight clings to the screen-hook;
Serenity reigns all round the spring brook.
The fragrance emanates from the planted strands;
The boatmen moor and cook foods on the sands.
The birds bicker for and spring on the sprigs;
The courtyard is swarmed with ephemerids;
Who has invented the opaque liquor?
A thousand cares might be melted in a beaker.

落　日

落日在簾鈎，
溪邊春事幽。
芳菲緣岸圃，
樵爨倚灘舟。
啅雀爭枝墜，
飛蟲滿院遊。
濁醪誰造汝，
一酌散千愁。

A Clear Evening After Rain

Through the evening village the winds sweep hard,
With shower spraying the recluse courtyard.
The grass basks itself in slanting sunbeam,
The river scenes loom on the bamboo screen.
My disarranged books who would care for?
I by myself shall repour the wine cupful.
Often do I hear gossips from all sides,
No wonder if an aged man here hides.

晚　晴

村晚驚風度，
庭幽過雨霑。
夕陽薰細草，
江色映疎簾。
書亂誰能帙，
盃乾可自添。
時聞有餘論，
未怪老夫潛。

Seeing Blossoms Alone Along the Riverside, Seven Versicles

I

The riverside flowers annoy me endlessly,
Nowhere can I complain but fumble crazily.
I go and visit my boon companion in south cottage,
He'd left a vacant bed ten days ago, for vintage.

II

The strands are wrapped in a cluster pavonine,
With stumbling steps I'm really shy of the spring shine.
Yet I can still compose the poem and drink the wine,
Grey headed, going to look after myself fine.

III

Mid quiet bamboos, by deep river, a few cots in sight,
Too noisy the red blossoms meddle with the white.
I know how to return the vernal day's favour —
To drink away my life with wines of the best flavour.

IV

The Little Town east is lost in clouds of flower,
The more adorable place is the Flora Tower.

江畔獨步尋花七絕句

江上被花惱不徹，
無處告訴只顛狂。
走覓南鄰愛酒伴，
經旬出飲獨空床。

稠花亂蕊裹江濱，
行步欹危實怕春。
詩酒當堪驅使在，
未須料理白頭人。

江深竹靜兩三家，
多事紅花映白花。
報答春光知有處，
應須美酒送生涯。

東望少城花滿烟，
百花高樓更可憐。

And who may cart the wine and fill the golden jugs,
And call for beauties dancing at feast, on the rugs?

V

By Monk Huang's pagoda the river runs east choppy,
The vernal zephyrs mellow me and make me sleepy.
No one but Nature owns the burst of peach blossom,
Which shall I love best, the pink one or the crimson?

VI

The numerous flowers o'erwhelm and bend the boughs,
And cloud the path leading to the Fourth Aunt of Huang's house.
At times the playing butterflies linger on and dance,
The carefree orioles delicately chirp and bounce.

VII

It's not that I love flowers and love them to death,
But that I fear they'll be gone and Dotage comes right forth.
Soon the multiflorous scene will fall like a shower,
I'd ask the buds not to hurry to burst into flower.

誰能載酒開金盞，
喚取佳人舞繡筵。

黃師塔前江水東，
春光懶困倚微風。
桃花一簇開無主，
可愛深紅愛淺紅？

黃四娘家花滿蹊，
千朵萬朵壓枝低。

留連戲蝶時時舞，
自在嬌鶯恰恰啼。

不是愛花即欲死，
只恐花盡老相催。
繁枝容易紛紛落，
嫩蕊商量細細開。

Poppy

All kinds of plants in spring-time vie for glory,
Poppy must have gained the finest dowry.
Rare as she is, she wears enticing rigs,
While the o'er-florid trees are full of twigs.
Such as peaches and plums e'erywhere profuse,
And can be transplanted, as though are refuse.
So precious creature you poppy have up grown,
And why all alone you live and wouldn't be known?

麗春

百草競春華，
麗春應最勝。
少須顏色好，
多漫枝條賸。
紛紛桃李枝，
處處總能移。
如何此貴重，
却怕有人知。

The Purple Mandarin-Ducks

The cage is designed to be spacious,
But would fray your plumes if you're impetuous.
Don't you feel lost when looking up to the cloud,
And in vain if for water you cry aloud.
Your colourful wings have been sheared shorter,
You can't fly high, e'en though become a bolter.
Neither falcon nor hawk you'll now care for;
Stay where you are then, and don't you get sore.

鸂鶒

故使籠寬織，
須知動損毛。
看雲莫悵望，
失水任呼號。
六翮曾經剪，
孤飛卒未高。
且無鷹隼慮，
留滯莫辭勞。

The Pied Duck

Waddling about the stone steps, you pied duck
Are too clean to be stained by filthy muck.
Your feathers are strong enough to show your might,
But cut too clearly the black part from white.
You know not jealousy to come from all sides,
Don't you do anything to start the green eyes!
There're rice and grain to feed your bill,
Be careful not to quack first and quack ill!

花　鴨

花鴨無泥滓，
階前每緩行。
羽毛知獨立，
黑白太分明。
不覺羣心妬，
休牽俗眼驚。
稻粱霑汝在，
作意莫先鳴。

Lines Written for Prefect Yan Wu When Once Again Seeing Him Off at the Courier Station of Fengji

We've gone a long way and here we'll bid adieu;
The mountains are green and void, but cling to you.
When shall we meet and drink a lot again?
Last night, in the moonlight, we walked hand in hand.
The counties would miss you and praise your deeds;
For three reigns, the Emperors crowned your feats.
I'll come back to my riverside village,
Secludedly living out my sear old age!

奉濟驛重送嚴公四韻

遠送從此別，
青山空復情。
幾時杯重把，
昨夜月同行。
列郡謳歌惜，
三朝出入榮。
江村獨歸處，
寂寞養殘生。

A Roamer's Night

Have I, a roamer, ever drifted into dreams?
The opaque autumnal sky never would turn blue!
Sieving through bamboo screens the setting moonlight streams;
Murmuring under my pillows the far-away river flows.
I have no means to manage my meal and clothes,
In the tight corner I depend upon my friend.
I shall write some sheets of paper to my old spouse,
So she will know why I'm not home and here detained.

客　夜

客睡何曾著，
秋天不肯明。
入簾殘月影，
高枕遠江聲。
計拙無衣食，
途窮仗友生。
老妻書數紙，
應悉未歸情。

A Roamer's Lodging

At last Dawn peeps at the autumn window under the eaves,
And in the whiffling winds the trees shed their leaves.
The sun rises from behind the cold mountain tops;
The river meanders away through the morning fog.
No one is left unheeded by our Imperial Court,
Only I am already an invalid of a sort.
It's the lees of my life and so many things have gone,
Wafting about, and I am like the fleabane down.

客　亭

秋窗猶曙色，
落木更天風。
日出寒山外，
江流宿霧中。
聖朝無棄物，
老病已成翁。
多少殘生事，
飄零任轉蓬。

News of the Government Troops Recapturing the Southern and Northern Parts of Ji

When comes to Sichuan news of the recapture
Of Ji, my tears stream down, wetting my vesture.
Wherefore then, should my spouse have her tortures?
I roll up my scrolls of poetry with raptures!
Drinking hard while singing aloud is fair in broad day;
The verdure spring will with us go home all the way.
Glide through Gorge Wu just as from Gorge Ba we'll start,
Then sail to Luoyang after from Xiangyang we'll part!

聞官軍收河南河北

劍外忽傳收薊北，
初聞涕淚滿衣裳。
却看妻子愁何在，
漫捲詩書喜欲狂。
白日放歌須縱酒，
青春作伴好還鄉。
即從巴峽穿巫峽，
便下襄陽向洛陽。

The Fledgeling Geese at the Prow of the Boat

The fledgeling geese are as yellow as wine;
I love them much when I hold a cup and dine.
Approaching, the prow their necks stretch to defy,
And swarming without line, they dazzle mine eye.
Last night, the rain has beaten their pinions,
Now they fret o'er the waves because of weak sinews.
Soon the dusk will veil the town and guests will go,
And what can you do with the fox —— the foe?

舟前小鵝兒

鵝兒黃似酒，
對酒愛新鵝。
引頸嗔船逼，
無行亂眼多。
翅開遭宿雨，
力小困滄波。
客散層城暮，
狐狸奈若何。

Late in the Year

I am a roamer far from home although it's late in the year,
While still the war is going on at the remote frontier.
The border tribes make clouds of dust when invading the Peak Snow, [1]
The riverain town is shaken by drums and horns they boom and blow.
Heaven and Earth are bleeding everyday, and to the King
Who will volunteer himself for service and the field win?
To fight the troublous times I shall not shrink from facing death,
Yet my brave heart can only be sore about my loneliness.

---

[1] In A.D. 763, the border tribes Tufan (吐蕃) invaded Sichuan Province. The Snow Peak (雪嶺) is the principal peak of Min Mountain (岷山), here it refers to Sichuan Province.

歲　暮

歲暮遠爲客，
邊隅還用兵。
烟塵犯雪嶺，

鼓角動江城。

天地日流血，
朝廷誰請纓？
濟時敢愛死？

寂寞壯心驚。

On the Tower

The blossoms, swaying near the tower, touch my feelings;
E'erywhere it is chaotic, and I stand by the railings.
Spring breathes along the River Jin, filling heaven and earth;
O'er the Mount Jade Piles, clouds are changeable since the world's birth.[1]
The North Star is e'erlasting; so is our country,
You robbers at the West Ranges don't try to us foray![2]
Here's the ancestral temple of the Late Emperor Liu,[3]
And in the gloom I sing a threnode for his due.

---

[1] River Jin and Mount Jade Piles are in Sichuan Province.
[2] "Robber" implies the border tribes Tufan.
[3] Liu Chan (see page 130) is also called Late Emperor Liu (劉後主). He was the last ruler of Kingdom Shu as it was subjugated by Jin (晋 , 265 – 420) dynasty.

登　樓

花近高樓傷客心，
萬方多難此登臨。
錦江春色來天地，
玉壘浮雲變古今。

北極朝廷終不改，
西山寇盜莫相侵。
可憐後主還祠廟，
日暮聊為梁甫吟。

The Home Going Wild Geese

When the chaotic world will settle down
That I may be home by the east sky-line?
Heart-broken, I see wild geese in a line,
Soaring northward from the riverside town.

雪華利祿寫

歸　雁

東來萬里客，
亂定幾年歸？
腸斷江城雁，
高高向北飛。

Two Versicles

I

The landscape smiles in the lagging, setting sun,
With scents of blooms and grass the spring winds run.
The swallows fly to pick the thawing sod,
In cozy sands the mandarin-ducks nod.

II

Birds're whiter against the waters blue,
And verdant mountains make their flowers glow.
The spring's fled from my eyes like scudding rack;
When shall I see the day I can go back?

雪華 利祿寫

絕句二首

一

遲日江山麗，
春風花草香。
泥融飛燕子，
沙暖睡鴛鴦。

二

江碧鳥逾白，
山青花欲然。
今春看又過，
何日是歸年。

Lodging at a Yamen

In General's Yamen, when autumn is chill,
  The kolanuts by a well stand in thrill.
Alone in the town by the riverside,
  I lodge with a waning candle light.
Like some soliloquised and sobbing groans,
  The horn in the long night dolefully croons.
Hanging high up above the mediation,
  The bright moon will invite whose appreciation?
How slowly the troublous times roll away,
  And from my brothers news is detained half way.
How desolate is the frontier pass all over,
  And how very hard the way for one to cover.
It has been a matter of ten years yet
  Since alone I suffered life's buffet.
Reluctantly I now remove to rest,
  On this branch, and find myself a cosy nest.

宿　府

清秋幕府井梧寒，

獨宿江城蠟炬殘。

永夜角聲悲自語，

中天月色好誰看？

風塵荏苒音書絕，

關塞蕭條行路難。

已忍伶俜十年事，

强移棲息一枝安。

Reflections in a Night While Travelling

The breezes stroke along the grassy strands,
The junk-mast tall and lone in darkness stands.
The speckled stars spread down to the fields wide,
The moon emerges from the rough river tide.
My pen has won me fame — has it been my will?
An official should not retire till old and ill![1]
What I am like that is everywhere wandering?
A gull between heaven and earth hovering.

---

[1] Tu Fu cherished ambitions more in politics than in writings, but he had never been successful in what he willed. In A.D. 765, when he was fifty-four years old, he resigned the position as General Yan Wu's (嚴武 , 726 – 765) advisor.

旅夜書懷

細草微風岸，
危檣獨夜舟。
星垂平野闊，
月湧大江流。
名豈文章著，
官應老病休。
飄飄何所似，
天地一沙鷗。

A Casual Versicle

The moon in the river shines within reach, it seems,
And in the deep night the lantern on the mast gleams.
Egrets huddle up like fists on the sandbank in sound sleep,
Behind the stern of the junk fish splash as they leap.

漫成一絕

江月去人只數尺，
風燈照夜欲三更。
沙頭宿鷺聯拳靜，
船尾跳魚撥剌鳴。

Spending the Night in the Room by the River

Along the mountain path creeps up the e'ening gloom,
Above the water-gate reposes my studying room.
The sleazy clouds float and lodge at the rocky caves,
The lonely moon undulates up and down in waves.
The cranes have calmed down after their pursuing flight;
The wolves ululate over their victims and fight.
The war presses me, sleepless, into worries' hold,
Unable as I am to do anything to right the world!

宿江邊閣

暝色延山徑，
高齋次水門。
薄雲巖際宿，
孤月浪中翻。
鸛鶴追飛靜，
豺狼得食喧。
不眠憂戰伐，
無力正乾坤。

Listening to the Songstress Yang

A matchless beauty sings a matchless song,
Her teeth are white and bright, and she stands long.
The hall is taken in sullen atmosphere,
The music soaring high to the blue sphere.
The pale moon shines the riverside city,
And she is floating in the night of serenity.
The dotard mourns for his declining years;
The brave's face is washed in bitter tears.
The jade cup is untouched for a long time,
I am lost to the precious pipes' chime.
Don't think that the audience are very tired,
All, fool and wise alike, their hearts have died.
Did e'er the ancient person outstanding
Wait for but one friend with good understanding?
I heard that there was a songster Qin Qing, [1]
Who had made the world give ear to listen.

---

[1] Qin Qing (秦青), a legendary songster whose songs can shake the trees and stop the clouds.

聽楊氏歌

佳人絕代歌，
獨立發皓齒。
滿堂慘不樂，
響下淸虛裏。
江城帶素月，
況乃淸夜起。
老夫悲暮年，
壯士淚如水。
玉杯久寂寞，
金管迷宮徵。
勿云聽者疲，
愚智心盡死。
古來傑出士，
豈待一知己。
吾聞昔秦青，
傾側天下耳。

Reflections in the Autumn, Eight Stanzas

I

The pearly dews depress and wilt the maple woods,
Wu Cliffs and Gorge are veiled in a haze of woes.
To heaven high the waves of Yangtze leap and bound,
The ominous clouds cloak the mountain pass to ground.
I'll weep for having twice seen asters bloom and die,
The lonely boat yet anchors my heart that'll home fly.
All scissors and rulers are busy for winter clothes,
And washing mallets beat at dusk in Baidi's alp blows.[1]

II

O'er lonely city Kuizhou the sun is slant and wane,
I nightly search where Capital is, by the Wain.
Indeed one'll cry when hearing the monkeys whine thrice,
A pity I miss the mission of "rafting skies". [2]

---

[1] Baidi (白帝), a mountain town near Wu Gorge (巫峽), of the Yangtze River in Sichuan province (四川省).

[2] It is said in the ancient folk tales that in the Eighth Moon every year there is a raft bound to the Milky Way. In another story, it is said that Chang Chien (張騫), the envoy of Emperor Wu of the Han dynasty (漢武帝), had been rafting there. Tu Fu here similized the Milky Way to the Capital Chang-an, where he longed to go back with General Yan Wu (嚴武). But the sudden death of the General (A.D. 765) failed him in what he expected.

秋興八首

一

玉露凋傷楓樹林，
巫山巫峽氣蕭森。
江間波浪兼天湧，
塞上風雲接地陰。
叢菊兩開他日淚，
孤舟一繫故園心。
寒衣處處催刀尺，
白帝城高急暮砧。

二

夔府孤城落日斜，
每依北斗望京華。
聽猿實下三聲淚，
奉使虛隨八月槎。

Disease prevents me from being promoted high;
Among the mounds on mountain tower bugles sigh.
Behold the moon above the ivy-mantled rocks,
Now shines the reeds on the river bank with silver shocks!

III

In alpenglow the town of thousand homes are in dreams,
In the tower by the river I daily sit to the greens.
Though another night is wasting fishers are still on float,
Though autumn comes the swallows flit still to and fro.
Like Kuang Heng, I've said something to the King, yet woe is me, [3]
Liu Xiang was learned in Classics, and I can't be. [4]
And my young schoolmates they all have fortune on their side;
In light furs, on fat steeds, through the Five Tombs they ride. [5]

---

[3] Kuang Heng (匡衡), an official of the Han dynasty. He sent a memorandum to Emperor Yuan (元帝) and was promoted for his good opinion. In A.D. 757, Tu Fu sent to Emperor Suzong (肅宗 , the Tang dynasty) a memorandum in defence of the discharged Prime Minister Fang Kuan (房琯), but he was degraded and nearly punished since the emperor thought it was offensive.

[4] Liu Xiang (劉向), a scholar of the Han dynasty. Emperor Xuan (宣帝) had appointed him to collate the Five Classics. Tu Fu here sighed that he had no such opportunities.

[5] Between Chang-an and Xianyang (咸陽) there were in the Han dynasty five great tombs where the demised emperors were buried. These were also the districts where lived the high officials and the rich. Tu Fu here alluded to those people of his contemporaries.

畫省香爐違伏枕，
山樓粉堞隱悲笳。
請看石上藤蘿月，
已映洲前蘆荻花。

三

千家山郭靜朝暉，
日日江樓坐翠微。
信宿漁人還泛泛，
清秋燕子故飛飛。
匡衡抗疏功名薄，

劉向傳經心事違。
同學少年多不賤，
五陵衣馬自輕肥。

IV

I hear that Chang-an is like a game of chess,
Events occured within the century are a mess.
The nobles' halls are rendered to new lords' hold,
High officials with vests are different from old. [6]
The gongs and drums at northern passes sound the hest,
The dispatch-riders hurry the chariots to the west.[7]
Yet here in autumn waters fish and dragons are lorn, [8]
Thinking of the Capital where I've lived I groan.

V

Facing the Zhongnan Hill the Penglai Palace rises high,
With brazen poles upholding the dew-plates to sky. [9]
One may descry the West Queen descending her Fairy Pond,
And Lao Zi passing Hangu Pass with purple mist around.[10]

---

[6] In A.D. 755 – 761, An Lushan and Shi Siming (see page 88) started war in rebellion against the Tang dynasty's ruler. It caused many changes happening in the Capital Chang-an.

[7] Still there were wars at the northern and western borders against the foreign tribes.

[8] Tu Fu here alluded to himself that in this far corner he was as lonely as the aquatics.

[9] In the palace of the emperor of the Han dynasty there had been built very tall brazen poles with plates on the tops for accepting dews for the emperor to drink. He thought it was something divine.

[10] The West Queen (西王母) is a Goddess in legendary tales. She lives in far west. Lao Zi (老子 , 604? B.C. – ?) was an ancient philosopher. It was said that when he came from east to the Hangu Pass (函谷關) there could be seen a purple mist with him. In these lines Tu Fu meant that so magnificent was the Penglai Palace (蓬萊宮) that from there one could see things far away.

四

聞道長安似奕棋，
百年世事不勝悲。
王侯第宅皆新主，
文武衣冠異昔時。
直北關山金鼓震，
征西車馬羽書馳。
魚龍寂寞秋江冷，
故國平居有所思。

五

蓬萊宮闕對南山，
承露金莖霄漢間。
西望瑤池降王母，
東來紫氣滿函關。

When pheasant-tail-fans move like clouds rolling away,
In a shining dragon-scaled-robe appears His Majesty.[11]
Now it's only a riverain dream in deep autumn-tide —
The days I waited for audience by Blue Chains side.[12]

VI

'Tween Qutang Gorge here and Winding River there,
Along ten thousand miles, haze bears the autumn air.[13]
There's Royal Lane from Calyx Chamber to Hibiscus,
The Park whereto from the borders came the news rebellious.[14]
The beaded screens and columns round the yellow swans,
Before the boats with ivory masts white gulls swarm.[15]
It's sad to look back at the place of dance and songs,

---

[11] An emperor used to wear a robe embroidered with dragon scales. There were big fans made of pheasant tail put before his throne as a screen. Whenever the emperor took his seat, the big fans were moved aside.

[12] Blue Chains (青瑣) was the name of the gate of a palace. The gate was carved with chain-work and painted blue.

[13] Qutang Gorge (瞿塘峽) is like the throat from where the Yangtze River flows out of Sichuan Province. The Winding River (曲江) was a pleasure resort in Chang-an. Tu Tu's thought linked the two places together.

[14] The Calyx Chamber (花萼樓) was a building in the Palace, from where there was a lane leading to the Lotus Park (芙蓉苑) by the Winding River. The lane was specially built with a tall wall at each side. Passing through the lane, Emperor Xuanzong (玄宗) with his concubine Yang (楊貴妃) frequented the Park and the news of the rebellion of An Lushan was reported to him at that time.

[15] Herein Tu Fu reflected the pompous views at the Winding River.

雲移雉尾開宮扇，
日繞龍鱗識聖顏。
一臥滄江驚歲晚，
幾回青瑣點朝班。

六

瞿塘峽口曲江頭，
萬里風烟接素秋。
花萼夾城通御氣，
芙蓉小苑入邊愁。
珠簾繡柱圍黃鵠，
錦纜牙檣起白鷗。
回首可憐歌舞地，

In Mid Qin, that e'er since ancient times, there were dynasts' towns.[16]

VII

The Kunming Lake is a merit of the Han dynasty,
And Emperor Wu's flags in my mind's eye display.[17]
The carved Spinster Maid stops spinning under the moon,
The Stone porpoise's scales seem to wave in Autumn's groan.[18]
The wild rices float on water like black-dyeing clouds,
The lotus pink petals fall as dews cool their pods.
Birds alone can pass the skyey mountain passes here,
I'm like a fisher since deep waters are e'erywhere.[19]

VIII

The way to Kunwu and Yusu was a twist to make,
The Purple Peak's penumbra fell in the Meipi Lake.
The parrots pecked at the fragrant paddy grain,
The phœnixes perched on the branches of the old plane.
The fairs greet'd each other, plucking the spring bloom,

---

[16] Mid Qin (秦中) was a district where several dynasties before Tang had settled their capitals. Tu Fu elliptically alluded here to the rises and falls in history.

[17] Kunming Lake (昆明池), south-west of Chang-an, was dredged by Emperor Wu of the Han dynasty for the manoeuvre of fleet action.

[18] The Spinster Maid (織女) and the porpoise are the stone sculptures by the Kunming Lake.

[19] Coming to himself from his reflections, Tu Fu found himself still in a bitter corner.

秦中自古帝王州。

七

昆明池水漢時功，
武帝旌旗在眼中。
織女機絲虛夜月，
石鯨鱗甲動秋風。

波漂菰米沉雲黑，
露冷蓮房墜粉紅。
關塞極天惟鳥道，
江湖滿地一漁翁。

八

昆吾御宿自逶迤，
紫閣峯陰入渼陂。
香稻啄餘鸚鵡粒，
碧梧棲老鳳凰枝。
佳人拾翠春相問，

With my good friends we oared even in the gloom.[20]
The day was when my magic pen did please the King,[21]
Bending my hoary head, I now but hope and sing.

---

[20] From Chang-an to Meipi (渼陂), by way of Kunwu (昆吾) and Yusu (御宿), more than a hundred li, there had been in the Han dynasty the Imperial Garden (上林苑), a famous place of scenery. Purple Peak (紫閣峯) was the peak of Zhongnan Hill (終南山).

[21] Tu Fu had written Three Fu (Prose-Poetry) of the Great Rites (《三大禮賦》) dedicated to the Emperor Xuanzong and was appreciated by the emperor.

仙侶同舟晚更移。
綵筆昔曾干氣象，
白頭吟望苦低垂。

The Odd Wild Goose

Without meal and drink, the odd wild goose flies;
Honking all the way, for missing the flock it cries.
Who cares that the shadow is diminishing
Into clouds thousands of miles away, and vanishing?
The vision seems still there when it disappears,
The songs, bearing deep sorrows, ring in the spheres.
Insensible to the world are the wild ducks;
They move restlessly with tumultuous quacks.

孤　雁

孤雁不飲啄，
飛鳴聲念羣。
誰憐一片影，
相失萬里雲。
望盡似猶見，
哀多如更聞。
野鴉無意緒，
鳴噪自紛紛。

The Gulls

The gulls play on the frigid river banks;
Vainly they live, they please themselves with pranks.
The day was when their snow-white feathers flapped,
Over the spring seedlings they freely tapped.
When in swarm the swarthy clouds come they must fall,
Or away along here and there with the squall.
But over the sea there are groups making fun,
While silhouetting against the glowing sun.

鷗

江浦寒鷗戲，
無他亦自饒。
却思翻玉羽，
隨意點春苗。
雲暗還須落，
風生一任飄。
幾羣滄海上，
清影日蕭蕭。

The Roe

Forever parted with the glazy brook,
I'm favoured to come to the table of feast.
No talent to serve as a hermit's beast;
How dare I have a grudge against the cook?
The vile world makes little of one's whole skin;
My slight fame involves me in disasters.
Those coroneted and garbed monsters,
All in a wink they gnaw and glut me in.

麂

永與清溪別，
蒙將玉饌俱。
無才逐仙隱，
不敢恨庖廚。
亂世輕全物，
微聲及禍樞。
衣冠兼盜賊，
饕餮用斯須。

A Night in a Chamber

The nights and days so swiftly flee at the end of the year,
At the corner of the earth, after snow, the cold, dark sky is clear.
In the dim owl-light the drums and bugles moan touchingly;
Between the Three Gorges the waves mirror the galaxy.
Several countrymen bewail that war is levied on,
And fishermen and woodsmen sing some alien folk-song.
Even Zhuge Liang and Gongsun Shu were but dust at last,[1]
How trivial to be sad at failures and from my kims apart.

---

[1] Zhuge Liang, see page 130. His military activities are described as legendary stories in the classic novel "The Story of The Three Kingdoms" (《三國演義》). Gongsun Shu (公孫述 A.D. ? – 36), an official of The Eastern Han dynasty, had made himself king of Sichuan Province, called himself "The White Emperor", but the rebellion was defeated and he was killed by Emperor Guangwu (光武帝).

閣夜

歲暮陰陽催短景，
天涯霜雪霽寒宵。

五更鼓角聲悲壯，
三峽星河影動搖。
野哭幾家聞戰伐，
夷歌數處起漁樵。
臥龍躍馬終黃土，
人事音書漫寂寥。

The Harvest-Moon, Two Stanzas

I

The mirror giant in my eyes dazzles bright,
My eagerness of going home can break a sword.
I have gone far away, like the fleabane in flight,
Too high to climb the Cassia Tree in the Round World.[1]
The angel's pathway seems to be paved with snow,
The arboreal creatures their feathers can be seen.
Looking up at the white Moon Hare from here below,
One can actually count the fluffy fur in the sheen.

II

A little way below the cliffs of Gorge Wu,
Yet still the moon bites at the Baidi City's walls.
The river darkens when She has a face of woe,
Half of the chamber lightens when She askew rolls.
The army pots are beaten, speeding Dawn to fall,
Moon Toad may find somewhere to lean on for your own!
Not only our Han soldiers now the bows they pull
To keep their guard under the beams that's fading soon.

---

[1] It is supposed in the fairy tales that in the moon there is a cassia tree of five thousand feet high which an immortal Wu Kang (吳剛) was condemned to chop at. He can never fell it since the kerfs will immediately mend themselves.

八月十五夜月 二首

一

滿目飛明鏡，
歸心折大刀。
轉蓬行地遠，
攀桂仰天高。
水路疑霜雪，
林棲見羽毛。
此時瞻白兔，
直欲數秋毫。

二

稍下巫山峽，
猶銜白帝城。
氣沉全浦暗，
輪仄半樓明。
刁斗皆催曉，
蟾蜍且自傾。
張弓倚殘魄，
不獨漢家營。

Another Poem to Master Wu [1]

Let my west neighbour come to my cottage garden and beat
Dates down from the trees, since she has no son, has nothing to eat.
Would she ever do that if it's not Poverty pressing behind?
So, sparing her from shyness, you must be gentle and kind.
There is no need of her shrinking from you —— my lodger from afar,
And it would be too callous to hurdle her out, to make a bar.
She has complained that taxes have made her poor to the bone,
And my tears wet my kerchief as I think war fires still burn.

---

[1] In A.D. 767, Tu Fu lent his Rangxi Cottage (瀼西草堂) to his relative Wu when he himself moved to live in Dongtun (東屯). This poem Tu Fu wrote him as a letter.

又呈吳郎

堂前撲棗任西鄰，
無食無兒一婦人。

不爲困窮寧有此？
祇緣恐懼轉須親。
即防遠客雖多事，

便插疏籬却任眞。
已訴徵求貧到骨，

正思戎馬淚霑巾。

Mounting

From heaven high the winds are whirring down with monkeys' whine,
And over the white sanded hursts the birds are cleaving fine.
The rimless forests shed their yellow leaves with rustles;
The ever flowing Yangtze on its way rolls and wrestles.
Autumn is chilling me — always a thousand-miles-roamer,
Alone mounting the mountain, and a lifelong sufferer.
I deeply loathe my rime-like temples as in these hard times,
Of late Senility yet forces me to give up wines.

登　高

風急天高猿嘯哀，

渚清沙白鳥飛迴。
無邊落木蕭蕭下，
不盡長江滾滾來。
萬里悲秋常作客，
百年多病獨登台。
艱難苦恨繁霜鬢，
潦倒新停濁酒杯。

Watching the Sword Dance Performed by the Pupil of the Elder Sister of Gongsun — with a Prelude

In the Tenth Moon, the nineteenth day, the second year of Dali Period, at the home of Yuanchi's, vice magistrate of Kuizhou, I saw the sword dance performed by the Twelfth Sister of Li from Linying. Being surprised at her splendid fencing, I asked her who her teacher was and she replied: "I am a pupil of the Elder Sister of Gongsun."

I was very young when in the fifth year of Kaiyuan Period. I remember I saw in Yan City Mistress Gongsun's sword dance, so crafty an rhythmical that none could be her superior of the day. At the beginning of Emperor Xuanzong Period, of all the musicians of or outside the Fair Spring and Pear Garden, the two court schools, Gongsun was the only one mastering the dance. She was then so beautiful in her embroidered dress, and now that even I am grey-haired, her pupil must be past her blooming years too! Having made out whom she has learned from, I know the likeness between the source and the effluent. And as the vicissitude of life worries me, I write the Sword Dance Poem.

Formerly, Zhang Xu of Wu County, a calligrapher, mastering in cursive handwriting on scrolls, had often seen at Ye

雪華利祿寫

觀公孫大娘弟子舞劍器行 並序

大曆二年，十月十九日，夔府別駕元持宅見臨潁李十二娘舞劍器，壯其蔚跂，問其所師，曰：“余公孫大娘弟子也。”開元五載，余尚童稚，記於郾城觀公孫氏舞劍器渾脫，瀏灕頓挫，獨出冠時。自高頭宜春、梨園二伎坊內人及外供奉，曉是舞者，聖文神武皇帝初，公孫一人而已。玉貌錦衣，況余白首；今茲弟子，亦匪盛顏。既辨其由來，知波瀾莫二。撫事慷慨，聊爲《劍器行》。往者吳人張旭，善草書書帖，數常於鄴縣見公孫大娘舞西河劍器，自此草書長進，豪蕩感激，即公孫可知矣。

County Mistress Gongsun's West River Sword Dance, and his writing was much improved, so unrestrained and emotional, that one may recall how marvellous Gongsun's art was.

In former days there was a fair of Gongsun family,
Her sword dance whene'er played always was a pageantry.
A mountain of audience was moved, with looks of dismay;
Even heaven and earth would heave and set their breath all day.
With flashes like the Archer Yi shot down the nine bright suns,[1]
And vigour like the Genii drove the dragons on cloud-way,
She rushed on, and it's the thunders rolling in a fury,
And when finished, it's the sea calmed down with smooth rays.
Her ruby lips and pearled sleeves both were gone for long,
Yet lately there's her pupil carrying her artistry.
The beauty of Linying has come to Baidi City,
Dancing the sword dance so gracefully and vividly.
I ask about her career and thus I know the story,
And the shifts and changes of life make me very dreary.
There were eight thousand maids in our deceased Emperor's court,
Among them, Mistress Gongsun's sword dance was e'er of the first.

---

[1] It is said in Chinese fairy tales that there had been ten suns in the sky and Archer Yi had shot nine of them down.

昔有佳人公孫氏，
一舞劍器動四方。
觀者如山色沮喪，
天地爲之久低昂。

㸌如羿射九日落，

矯如羣帝驂龍翔。
來如雷霆收震怒，
罷如江海凝清光。

絳脣珠袖兩寂寞，
晚有弟子傳芬芳。
臨穎美人在白帝，
妙舞此曲神揚揚。
與余問答既有以，
感時撫事增惋傷。
先帝侍女八千人，

公孫劍器初第一。

As easily as one turns one's hand, fifty years passed;
The royal houses were dimmed by chaotic clouds of dust.
All court actors were separated like smoke gone with gust,
Only the dancer's shadow gestures in the cold sunlight.
Trees have arched o'er the Tomb on Mount Jinsu, south of the crest,[2]
At the Stone City, near the Qutang Gorge, grasses are withered.[3]
And now, when sumptuous feasts with music and songs are finished,
Joy gives place to Sorrow and the moon is rising east.
Not knowing where she is going, I linger with my calloused feet
Printing among the desolate hill, and griefs swirl in my chest.

---

[2] Jinsu (金粟), a mountain where there was the tomb of Emperor Xuanzong who, and his son Emperor Suzong at the same time, died in the year 762.

[3] Stone City, refers to Baidi City.

五十年間似反掌，
風塵澒洞昏王室。
梨園弟子散如烟，
女樂餘姿映寒日。
金粟堆南木已拱，

瞿唐石城草蕭瑟。

玳筵急管曲復終，

樂極哀來月東出。
老夫不知其所往，

足繭荒山轉愁疾。

Moon and Stars Over the River, Two Stanzas

I

A sudden downpour cleans the autumn night,
The golden streams of moon illume the stars.
The Milky-Way forever shines so white,
The river, usually a crystal glass,
Reflects the scattered pearls, glistening,
When the great mirror floats up to the skies.
As the night thickens, she goes glimmering,
When dews are cooling and moistening the wilds.

II

The moon and stars o'er the river take leave
Of the misty boat and the windy railing.
When cocks' crows bringing dawn into relief.
The egrets come to bathe in brook hyaline.
Who planted the Cassia in the moon plot?[1]
Where would she go showing up her round face?
As sorrows crowd upon me I cannot,
But in other night I'll admire her grace.

---

[1] See page 208.

江邊星月 二首

一

驟雨清秋夜，
金波耿玉繩。
天河元自白，
江浦向來澄。
映物連珠斷，
緣空一鏡升。
餘光隱更漏，
況乃露華凝。

二

江月辭風檻，
江星別霧船。
鷄鳴還曙色，
鷺浴自晴川。
歷歷竟誰種，
悠悠何處圓？
客愁殊未已，
他夕始相鮮。

Travelling South

Along the peach-bloomed shore flows the spring tide,
Reading the maple trees the cloudy sails glide.
For life's sake, I'm always a refugee,
Travelling far away, my tears ne'er cease.
A doddering invalid, I go south,
Still yearning for the King's kindness, I look north.
For a lifetime I have bitterly sung,
Ne'er have I met a good understanding one!

南　征

春岸桃花水，
雲帆楓樹林。
偷生長避地，
適遠更沾襟。
老病南征日，
君恩北望心。
百年歌自苦，
未見有知音。

Along the Yangtze and Han River

Along the Yangtze and Han River I roam,
A stale pedant, I think of going home.
A sheet of cloud floats far to the unknown,
And all through the night I'm lone with the moon.
I'm like the setting sun, but with a heart young still,
And autumn winds fan me rallying from ill.
In ancient days they kept the aged horse,
Not necessarily because it could run a long course.

江　漢

江漢思歸客，
乾坤一腐儒。
片雲天共遠，
永夜月同孤。
落日心猶壯，
秋風病欲蘇。
古來存老馬，
不必取長途。

Swallows Coming to My Boat

Since I strayed to Hunan Province one year has fled by;
Once more the swallows, pecking mud for nests, swiftly fly.
Having entered my old home, with me they made acquaintance;
Today, at the spring feast, they look at me from a distance.
I pity them for building abodes everywhere,
It's no different from wandering in the world here and there!
They twitter for a while on the tall mast and then take wing,
Flitting through blossoms or shaving waters, my tears they win!

燕子來舟中作

湖南爲客動經春，
燕子銜泥兩度新。
舊入故園嘗識主，

如今社日遠看人。
可憐處處巢君室，
何異飄飄託此身。
暫語船檣還起去，
穿花貼水益霑巾。

Coming Across Li Guinian in Jiangnan[1]

I saw you now and then in Prince Qi's house,
And heard your songs in Courtier Cui's grand rooms.
When sights are fine in the Land of the South,
I meet you again in a shower of blooms.

---

[1] Li Guinian, a famous musician in Tu Fu's time. He was often invited by the noblemen in his youth, but in 770, several months before Tu Fu's last days, when they met again, they were both roaming in Jiangnan, the vast territory south of the Yangtze River.

江南逢李龜年

岐王宅裏尋常見，
崔九堂前幾度聞。
正是江南好風景，
落花時節又逢君。